THE 5 YEARS BEFORE YOU RETIRE

Retirement Planning When You Need It the Most

UPDATED EDITION

EMILY GUY BIRKEN

Adams Media

New York London Toronto Sydney New Delhi

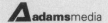

Adams Media
An Imprint of Simon & Schuster, Inc.
100 Technology Center Drive
Stoughton, MA 02072

Copyright © 2014, 2021 by Simon & Schuster, Inc.

This Adams Media trade paperback edition May 2021

ADAMS MEDIA and colophon are trademarks of Simon & Schuster.

For information about special discounts for bulk purchases, please contact Simon & Schuster Special Sales at 1-866-506-1949 or business@simonandschuster.com.

The Simon & Schuster Speakers Bureau can bring authors to your live event. For more information or to book an event contact the Simon & Schuster Speakers Bureau at 1-866-248-3049 or visit our website at www.simonspeakers.com.

Interior design by Priscilla Yuen

Manufactured in the United States of America

8 2023

Library of Congress Cataloging-in-Publication Data
Names: Birken, Emily Guy, author.
Title: The 5 years before you retire, updated edition / Emily Guy Birken.
Description: Updated edition. | Avon, MA: Adams Media, 2021. | Includes bibliographical references and index.
Identifiers: LCCN 2021000302 | ISBN 9781507213605 (pb) | ISBN 9781507213612 (ebook)
Subjects: LCSH: Retirement income--Planning. | Retirement--Planning. | Finance, Personal.
Classification: LCC HG179 .B489 2021 | DDC 332.024/014--dc23
LC record available at https://lccn.loc.gov/2021000302

ISBN 978-1-5072-1360-5
ISBN 978-1-5072-1361-2 (ebook)

DEDICATION

For my father, Jim Guy: mensch extraordinaire, talented financial planner, and Renaissance man. I wish I could have seen you beaming as you read this.

ACKNOWLEDGMENTS

This book could not have come to be without the help of many kind and knowledgeable friends and experts:

Thank you to Peter Archer and Brendan O'Neill, my editors at Adams Media, for giving me another crack at *5 Years*. This book means so much to me, and I'm so glad to be able to update it for a new audience.

In addition, I would like to thank the bloggers at *Wise Bread* (WiseBread.com), as well as the wonderful FinCon community that has done so much to help shape my financial writing career. Julie Jason, president of Jackson, Grant Investment Advisers, Inc., was kind enough to answer my many questions and point me in the right direction on more than one occasion. Thank you for taking the time to help me.

Finally, I'd like to thank my husband, Jayme. Thank you for patiently listening to me rant about financial issues in retirement for over a decade now—and for always keeping your eyes from glazing over.

CONTENTS

PART 3 HOME, FAMILY, AND OTHER CONSIDERATIONS 153

PREFACE TO THE REVISED AND UPDATED EDITION

Seven years ago, when I first wrote *The 5 Years Before You Retire*, it was my mission to create a comprehensive retirement guide that could help anyone understand the steps they needed to take to reach a secure and fulfilling retirement. Finance can often be an intimidating and opaque subject, and I wanted this book to offer reassurance and clarity, which I think it did.

Of course, even the clearest of financial guides will eventually become outdated. In the past seven years, a number of things have changed that have affected both the information in this book and the process of planning for retirement. Just to name a few, the changes to healthcare, the passage of a new tax bill, the changes to Social Security, and the profound economic effects of the coronavirus have all impacted the way near-retirees plan for their next act. Revising and updating this book has allowed me to provide my readers with the most accurate and up-to-the-minute information about the legislative rules that affect their retirement.

The past seven years have also seen a number of financial changes. From the recovery of the housing market to the rise (and fall) of cryptocurrency, and from the record-breaking highs of the stock market to the coronavirus-related changes to our economy, the market has been through a long, strange trip over the past decade. Though market fluctuation is inevitable, this kind of roller coaster deeply affects how we all feel about investing, and we see that emotional reaction reflected in our retirement planning strategies. As with the first edition of *5 Years*, this updated version will help you to plan and stick to a financial strategy that will see you through market fluctuations without panicking.

Finally, there have been several personal experiences in my life in the past seven years that have helped me better understand some important retirement planning strategies. My personal experiences with estate planning, investing, and researching long-term-care insurance have all deepened my knowledge of these topics. This new understanding has helped me see more nuances and offer more accurate advice to those who are planning their retirement, and you will find this reflected in the pages of this edition.

Despite what anyone in red suspenders and slicked-back hair might tell you, no financial analyst, adviser, or author can tell you exactly what to expect as you plan for your retirement. However, even though there is no crystal ball, you can count on the steps set out in this book. Each chapter guides you through the decisions and actions you will need to take to reach a secure retirement. The retirement planning syllabus at the end of each chapter, and the full syllabus in Appendix B, will help you know when to take which actions as you prepare for retirement. In addition, the new-to-this-edition Retirement Readiness Checklist in Appendix A can give you a bird's-eye view of your retirement preparation so you can pinpoint which parts of your plan need attention.

When you have finished reading this new revised and updated edition, you will feel confident about your plan and ready to tackle your retirement to-do list, with all the most current information at your fingertips.

Welcome to the five years before you retire. I'm excited to be your guide for this transition.

Emily Guy Birken

INTRODUCTION

So, here you are. You've worked for decades, squirreling money away, planning for that legendary time that is retirement. You're finally about five years away—close enough to it that you can practically taste it.

And yet…you're worried.

- Do I have enough saved?
- Will my finances recover from the economic downturn of 2020?
- How do I handle being laid off late in my career?
- What taxes will I have to pay?
- What, in my lifestyle, will I have to cut back?
- Should I sell the house and move somewhere cheaper?
- What happens if I get sick?

Sure, you might have read through the metric ton of retirement books out there. But every book you pick up seems to be geared toward someone other than you. Some are aimed at the twenty- and thirty-somethings who are just starting to save for retirement. Others are intended for retirees whose Social Security checks are insufficient and are trying to avoid living on cat food. But what about you? How can you find out what you need to do in these last few years before retirement to make sure your life post-career is financially comfortable and fulfilling?

That's what this book is for.

Rather than muddle through the myriad decisions you will have to make in the next few years, this book will help you to determine a clear, safe path. I'll guide you through the various choices available and explain the elements that make up a secure retirement.

Over the next thirteen chapters, I will go over every aspect of your upcoming retirement—including some issues that may not have occurred to you. In addition to discussing the dollars and cents of creating a sustainable retirement income, I'll lead you through the intricacies of finding the right financial planner and figuring out Social

Security and Medicare, and explain how taxes will affect your retirement, estate planning, retirement living, healthcare, and budgeting.

Why Five Years?

Why five years out? Why not ten? Twenty? Or, for that matter, one? Many books about retirement planning suggest that you start saving for retirement virtually from the moment you get a job. They point out that it's a far better problem to realize that you have more money than you expected upon retirement than too little. In general, they're right about this, but I can't help but think they're a bit unrealistic. Almost no one starts retirement planning at age twenty. There are too many other things to consider at that point. You're at the beginning of your career, and you're probably starting to think about big, life-changing decisions: getting married, buying a house, having children, and so on.

Five years from retirement seems realistic to me because that's the point at which it really hits home to most people that they're actually going to retire in the foreseeable future. Five years is also a good time frame—as this book will make clear—for accomplishing the various things you need to have done before you kick the dust of your workplace from your feet.

How to Use This Book

This book is set up so that you can get a great deal out of it whether you start on page 1 and read through to the end, or you simply read a chapter here and there as you encounter various issues in your retirement planning.

Each chapter offers you a checklist to help you apply the chapter's concepts to your own life. The next few years will be exciting ones as you start the transition from career to retirement. Don't let the choices you have to make paralyze you. With the information in this book, you'll be able to take a proactive role in your retirement and place yourself firmly in the driver's seat for the next chapter of your life.

1

The Nitty-Gritty of Retirement Finances

CHAPTER 1

How Far Away Are You?
A Realistic Definition of Retirement

WHAT YOU'LL LEARN IN THIS CHAPTER

Reaching a secure retirement can feel a little intimidating. How do you figure out how much you need? The process for achieving a stable retirement may seem opaque, but this chapter will break down the specific financial calculations you will need to make to figure out how well prepared you are for retirement, and you will learn what you need to do to prepare financially for your retirement.

Retirement used to be a fairly simple proposition. After working thirty-five or forty years for the same employer, your bosses gave you a gold-plated watch and a goodbye luncheon. You started spending your days at the golf course, enjoying the grandkids, or puttering around the house, all while collecting your pension and healthcare benefits from your loyal former employer.

Unfortunately, this is no longer what retirement looks like. Defined benefit pension plans—where your employer foots the bill for your retirement—are going the way of the dodo. According to the Bureau of Labor Statistics, as of 2018 only 17 percent of workers in the private sector had access to a traditional defined benefit pension. If your employer offers you any kind of assistance in preparing for retirement, it's likely to come in the form of a 401(k) defined contribution retirement plan.

The 1978 introduction of Section 401(k) to the Internal Revenue Code gave employers a method of helping their workers save for the future while putting the burden of saving and investing on the individual worker. This shifted the investment risk from the employer to the employee. The upside of this is that you have much more control over your retirement savings and income than ever before. Of course, you might have little to fall back on if you didn't save enough or if the market takes a nosedive at the wrong time, as anyone who planned to retire in the spring of 2020 can tell you. Contemplating twenty or thirty years of retirement without enough money is a pretty scary prospect and is the number one worry among soon-to-be retirees.

Thankfully, this is not your parents' retirement. You hold the reins when it comes to your investment and savings decisions, and you have the ability to return to work if necessary in order to keep both money concerns and boredom at bay. Where retirement might have once signaled the beginning of old age, it is now the next exciting chapter in your life.

Getting Ready for Retirement in the Next Five Years

Most people prefer not to think about how to handle retirement income. This is partially because any calculations on how much money you'll need for retirement requires an end date—and who wants to start speculating on when their retirement will "end"?

RETIREMENT INCOME RULE OF THUMB

Most retirement experts recommend replacing 80 percent of the value of your paycheck in order to maintain your lifestyle. Each year of your retirement, increase that amount by 3 percent to account for inflation.

Thankfully, you don't need to make such grim predictions in order to have a well-funded retirement. To make sure you're in a good position to start the transition from work to retirement, you'll need to figure out your monthly expenses, the amount of retirement income you can count on (including Social Security and any pensions you may be eligible for), the size of your retirement nest egg, and the effects of interest on your money.

STEP ONE

Fill in your information on the following table.

WORKSHEET 1-1:

How Much Do I Have (and How Much Will I Need)?

CALCULATE WHAT YOUR MONTHLY EXPENSES IN RETIREMENT WILL BE	
Rent/Mortgage	$
Car Payment	$
Groceries and Household Items	$
Dining Out	$
Gasoline	$
Public Transportation	$
Electric Bill	$
Gas Bill	$
Water Bill	$
Trash Pickup Bill	$
Cable/Internet/Satellite Bill	$
Telephone Bill	$
Cell Phone Bill	$
Credit Card/Loan Payments	$
Personal Care (Haircuts, etc.)	$
Health/Dental Insurance	$
Subscriptions	$
Memberships	$
Property Taxes	$
Homeowner's Insurance	$
Car Insurance	$
Miscellaneous	$
TOTAL	$

STEP TWO

Multiply that number by twelve in order to determine your yearly retirement expenses:

.... × 12 = ...

STEP THREE

Look up the amount of money you can count on from Social Security and any pensions you may have. (We will get into the details of Social Security benefits in Chapter 5. For now, you can use the Social Security Administration's Retirement Estimator at www.socialsecurity .gov/estimator in order to get a rough idea of how much to expect in retirement.)

CATEGORY	MONTHLY BENEFIT
Social Security	$
Pension(s)	$
TOTAL	$

STEP FOUR

Multiply that number by twelve in order to determine your guaranteed yearly retirement income:

.... × 12 = ...

STEP FIVE

Subtract your yearly guaranteed income from your yearly expenses. This will give you the amount of money you will need to bring in through alternate retirement vehicles in order to cover all of your expenses: This is what the AARP's Julie Jason refers to as the "income gap," and I'll use that term throughout this book.

STEP SIX

To estimate how much you will need in order to retire comfortably, divide your income gap by the savings return factor in the following table, which appears courtesy of Julie Jason, author of *The AARP Retirement Survival Guide.* This table assumes a thirty-year retirement and offers you four potential rates of return. Find the rate of return you are most comfortable assuming (3 percent would provide you with the most conservative estimate, and 6 percent would provide you with the most aggressive estimate), and use the corresponding return factor for your calculation.

ASSUMED ANNUAL RETURN ON SAVINGS	RETURN FACTOR
3% Annual After-Tax Return on Savings	Divide by 3.30%
4% Annual After-Tax Return on Savings	Divide by 3.85%
5% Annual After-Tax Return on Savings	Divide by 4.40%
6% Annual After-Tax Return on Savings	Divide by 5.00%

STEP SEVEN

Now do the calculations based upon your own numbers (your income gap divided by your savings return factor):

.... / .... = ...

This is a rough estimate of how much money you will need in order to retire. We will talk in much more detail later in the book about how to determine your specific needs and how to best invest and withdraw your money in order to ensure your money will last. For now, we'll just use your nest egg estimate as a rough measurement to see how much of a shortfall (if any) you will be facing between what you have already saved and what you will need.

STEP EIGHT

Look up the amount of your current savings: ....
Subtract that amount from the number you calculated in Step Seven:

....

This is your rough projected shortfall, and knowing this number can help you decide the best course of action for your retirement savings over the next five years.

CHAPTER 1 TAKEAWAYS

☑ The vast majority of workers (83 percent) cannot count on a defined benefit pension program from their employers. You will have to set aside money for your retirement if you hope to enjoy a secure second chapter like your parents and grandparents had.

☑ Calculating your retirement income needs will start with your current monthly expenditures. Multiply that number by twelve to determine your annual expenses.

☑ Compare your annual expenses to the amount of money you can count on from Social Security or other guaranteed retirement income.

☑ The difference between your annual expenses and your guaranteed income is your income gap.

☑ Dividing your income gap number by a return factor between 3.3 percent (for a conservative estimate) and 5.0 percent (for an aggressive estimate) will give you a rough estimate of how much money you will need to retire.

☑ Subtracting your current savings from your rough estimate tells you how much you still need to save before retirement.

CHAPTER 2

Saving and Budgeting for the Next Five Years: Maximizing Your Savings

WHAT YOU'LL LEARN IN THIS CHAPTER

An important part of preparing for your retirement in the next five years is making sure your financial choices are aligned with your goals and values. This chapter will teach you how to prioritize your spending, savings, and investing for retirement to make sure you reach your goals. You'll also understand the importance of pre-retirement budgeting, and how you can use your budget to help you maximize your retirement savings. Finally, you will learn various methods for creating your budget using online programs, software, or mobile apps.

Even if the shortfall amount that you came up with in Worksheet 1–1 feels depressingly high, remember that you have time to catch up. Not only do you have the five years between now and your retirement target date; you also don't need to stop growing your nest egg when you end your career. Your investments can continue to grow and take advantage of the magic of compound interest even when you are no longer working. If you plan to set aside some of your money to grow over the next twenty years, you can afford to invest in more aggressive investments that can offer potentially better rates of return. This asset allocation strategy is called the bucket method, and we'll discuss how it works in detail in Chapter 3.

But even if you plan to strategically invest your money in such a way, it's smarter to save now to make up as much of your shortfall as possible. That's because any investment decision you make is based on educated guesses, since no one can know the future. You have to remember that you cannot control how the market performs, but you can control how much you save. If you are looking at a significant shortfall between where you are now and where you need to be in five years (basically, if you need to save a great deal more than you otherwise would for each of the five years left in your career), then it's time to look for creative ways to put away extra cash.

If the amount of money you need to put aside over the next five years rivals the GDP of an island nation, you might want to skip ahead to Chapter 13: If You Don't Have Enough Saved. If, however, you just need to beef up your savings somewhat, here are some tried-and-true methods for feeding the retirement piggy bank.

Maximize Your Employer's 401(k) Contribution Match

Get your employer's maximum contribution match on your 401(k). Many employers offering defined contribution plans (the generic term for 401(k) and 403(b) plans) will provide employees with a contribution match up to a certain percentage of salary.

If you can take advantage of a matching program, the most common match gives you 50 cents for every dollar contributed up to 6 percent of your salary. Some generous companies will match every dollar of your contribution up to 3–6 percent. Not maxing out this kind of matching program is akin to leaving free money on the table.

Maximize Retirement Contributions

Make certain you are maximizing your retirement contributions. Both your employer-sponsored defined contribution plan (i.e., your 401(k)) and your Individual Retirement Account (IRA) have yearly contribution limits that you should strive to meet every year until you retire. The current contribution limits for 2021 are $19,500 for defined contribution plans and $6,000 for IRAs. These investment vehicles offer unique tax benefits that can help many investors do more with their money. (In this section, I will be talking exclusively about traditional

401(k)s and IRAs. The Roth version of these retirement accounts offers different tax benefits, and I will discuss in detail those differences and how to maximize them in Chapter 6, along with further details about the tax implications of traditional 401(k)s and IRAs.)

One of the biggest benefits of a traditional defined contribution plan and traditional IRA is their tax-deferred status. In both cases, you can deduct your contributions from your yearly taxes—thereby lowering your current tax burden—also described as funding your account with pre-tax dollars.

This tax benefit can be a major boon for workers, especially those nearing retirement, as it can help free up more money in the budget to go toward the all-important retirement savings. You will, of course, eventually have to pay taxes on these accounts, although the money in both 401(k)s and IRAs grows tax-deferred, meaning you do not have to pay taxes when your account gains capital or earns dividend income. However, when you withdraw funds from your tax-deferred retirement account, you will owe ordinary income tax on your distribution (another word for withdrawal).

Don't forget that there are income limits on who can deduct IRA contributions from their taxes. As of 2021, the deduction is on a sliding scale for single filers earning a yearly income of between $66,000 and $76,000 (i.e., it ranges from a full deduction of the entire contribution amount to no deduction). If you file as a single person and make more than $76,000, you cannot take advantage of the tax deduction. For married couples filing jointly, the range is between $105,000 and $125,000.

No matter what your income is, however, it's important to stay abreast of the contribution limits you may take advantage of each year. The limits go up for workers who have reached age fifty, giving them an opportunity to "catch up" if they were not diligent about maximizing their contributions each year earlier in their careers. Currently, the over-fifty crowd can contribute up to $26,000 a year to their 401(k)s and $7,000 to their IRAs—$6,500 and $1,000 more than their younger counterparts can contribute. In addition, the IRS readjusts both the general and "catch-up" contribution limits every few years, so make sure you are always completely funding these investment vehicles. This is an excellent way to prepare financially for retirement.

Reduce Your Expenses

Although every family's circumstances and budget are different, there are several money-saving options that are particularly attractive and doable for soon-to-be retirees.

- Downsize your home. The home where you raised your family may be full of wonderful memories, but it's probably larger than you currently need. Moving to a smaller home could also include a move to an area with lower property taxes (empty nesters don't need to worry about good school districts anymore). In addition, any equity you get out of your home through such a sale could beef up your retirement savings.

- If you are still paying your mortgage, you can reduce your housing expenses through a refinance.

- Take in a roommate or boarder. Sharing your home is not just for college kids. Splitting housing and utility expenses with an additional person can free up a great deal of money. While sharing your home may feel a little awkward at first, finding a roommate or boarder who is a good fit will not only improve your finances, it can also potentially add to your enjoyment. We all saw how well it worked for the Golden Girls. Sites like Silvernest.com and SharingHousing.com can help both homeowners and homeseekers find each other.

- Become a one-car household. It's likely your parents made do with only one car while you were growing up, and you can certainly re-create that standard of living. Selling one car will potentially mean one less car payment, cheaper insurance, less maintenance, and less gas consumption.

- Reduce your restaurant and entertainment expenses. Americans got a crash course in this kind of expense reduction during the coronavirus quarantine. One of the silver linings of the stay-at-home order was how it helped us to pinpoint exactly which dining and entertainment experiences we missed most and which ones we'd be happy to forgo to save money. Cutting back on the fun expenses you feel "meh" about can help you save money while protecting the fun experiences you value the most.

- Cancel your unused subscriptions. Many companies make their money through subscription services that their customers no longer use. According to a 2013 study by industry analysts Aite Group, consumers spend $14.3 billion on these charges each year. These ongoing fees, known in the industry as gray charges, account for 233 million transactions per year. The charges are legal, and rely on the fact that most people do not pay close attention to their statements. The DIY method of canceling unused subscriptions is simple: Look through your credit card and bank statements to identify the offending gray charges, and call to cancel the unused subscriptions. If you'd rather not spend the time yourself, however, apps like Trim (www.asktrim.com) and Truebill (www.truebill.com) will cancel unused subscriptions for you.

Ask the Expert

Ryan Guina, finance blogger at *Cash Money Life* (www.cashmoneylife.com), agrees that saving for retirement should be one of the two big financial priorities for those nearing retirement. The other one is paying off consumer debt, as that will ensure that you keep all of your retirement income, rather than owing some each month to a creditor. Ryan gives the following advice for making your retirement goals a reality: "There are often competing financial goals to consider in the years leading up to retirement, such as paying off debt, paying for your child's college or wedding, and increasing retirement savings. While each financial situation is different, you can never go wrong with the two-pronged approach of eliminating debt and saving more for retirement. I would prioritize these as follows:

1. Saving up to the employer match in a 401(k) plan, pension, or other employer-sponsored retirement plan.
2. Eliminating consumer debt.
3. Maxing out a Roth IRA.
4. Maxing out your employer-sponsored retirement plan(s)."

By completing these goals in the order that Ryan recommends, you will make the most of your money. Taking advantage of the employer match in your employer-sponsored plan means that you may have as much as doubled your money. Whatever consumer debt you have is probably charging you higher interest than you could earn through any investments, so eliminating all of your consumer debt will help your money go further and save you a great deal of money over time. If you have money left over, maxing out your IRA makes more sense, as there is a lower maximum threshold. Ryan also recommends having a Roth IRA for the purposes of tax diversification—that is, just as you want to make sure your assets reflect a diversity of investments, you will want your taxes to be due at various times so that you are not overwhelmed by paying taxes all at once. We'll cover this idea in more detail in Chapter 6.

Finally, if you have covered the first three financial bases, go ahead and max out your employer-sponsored retirement plan. If you have limited funds for retirement planning, following Ryan's plan for your money is a smart way to decide where your money should go and when. For those individuals who have enough money left over after following Ryan's plan, there is still more you can do to get yourself set up for a comfortable retirement: Work on eliminating your mortgage, as housing costs are often the biggest living expense and should be minimized in retirement. Follow that up by making investments in taxable investment accounts, which are the only investments available to those individuals who have maxed out their 401(k)s and IRAs. If you can enter retirement with no consumer debt, maxed-out tax-deferred and tax-free retirement accounts, no mortgage, and a few taxable investment accounts under your belt, then you'll be sitting pretty for the next stage of your life.

Budgeting Before Retirement

"That's great," you may be saying. "Now I know that I need to save more and max out my retirement accounts in the next five years. But how do I go about doing that?"

In a word: budgeting.

Before you recoil in horror at the idea of keeping track of every dollar that passes through your hands, remember that creating, maintaining, and periodically tweaking your budget is a vital aspect of preparing for retirement. You may be able to get away with ignoring your money choices while you are working full-time and bringing home a good salary, but maintaining that same level of money ignorance as you prepare for retirement is a good way to ensure your plans and finances go off the rails. Knowing how you spend your money will allow you to make the decisions that make the difference between a fulfilling and well-funded retirement and learning to enjoy meals of crackers with ketchup. If you have never kept a budget before, now is the time to start, and you will find that it is a lot less painful than you may fear.

We'll discuss in great detail in Chapter 11 how to create and maintain a household budget on a retirement income. What I want to discuss here is how to construct a budget in the years prior to retirement. The main difference between the two budgets is that in a household budget, because you are still drawing a full-time salary, you have some wiggle room. Even if you do not calculate everything down to the penny, there's no need to really worry since you'll be getting your next paycheck within a couple of weeks. Because you can count on your income, you do not necessarily have to be precise with your finances. Retirees often refer to their "fixed income." That's because there is a great deal less wiggle room when you simply cannot spend more than your monthly allotment. All that said, pre-retirement and post-retirement budgeting does not have to be frightening.

Budget Basics

All any budget really does is track two things: where your money comes from and where it goes. It is then up to you to incorporate the budgeting action step: Spend less than you earn. Spending less is not difficult since we all have expenses that we can easily do without or modify to be less expensive. But until you know exactly what you're bringing in and where it's going, it can be almost impossible to figure out where to cut your spending. So the start of the budgeting process is to determine your income and your outflow.

WHY I HATE THE "LATTE FACTOR"

The "Latte Factor" was coined by David Bach, who points out that small, regular expenses add up to large amounts. For instance, if you buy a $5 cup of coffee five days a week, you are wasting $1,300 per year on coffee. While I have no quibble with Bach's math, I feel like it misses the point. People who spend $5 on coffee every day are probably not paying close attention to where any of their money goes. Cutting out small luxuries like this will not make a dent in the finances of someone who is not keeping track of her money, since she is unlikely to save up all those five-dollar bills until she has $1,300 to bank. All this tip does is make people feel guilty for enjoying small luxuries. Having a realistic budget ensures that you are conscious of where you are spending your money—even if that includes your Starbucks habit.

TRACKING YOUR INCOME

While you are still working, tracking your income will be the easiest part of creating your budget. Unless you work as a freelancer or otherwise have irregular or variable income, it's simple to look through your pay stubs to find out how much you bring in each month. However, you will also want to include any other sources of income such as alimony, child support, rental income, disability checks, and dividends from stocks. To start, gather all of your income records for the last month (or year, for any income you receive irregularly), and record them in Worksheet 2–1: Tracking Your Income (courtesy of Tere Stouffer). You will record your net income—that is, the amount of money you see from each check after taxes, 401(k) contributions, union dues, or any other automatic withdrawals are removed. For this worksheet, you will record your net income based on how often you are paid:

- Weekly
- Biweekly
- Semimonthly—this is when you always receive two paychecks per month, even in months with five weeks; for instance, you might be paid on the first and fifteenth of every month

- Monthly
- Quarterly—most likely this will include quarterly dividends from any stocks you own
- Semiannually—you may receive some nonwork-related income payments semiannually
- Annually—you can include any bonuses that you know you will receive each year; if your bonuses are dependent on either your or your company's performance, do not include them in your income calculations

WORKSHEET 2-1:

Tracking Your Income

SOURCE OF INCOME	AMOUNT	MULTIPLY BY	ANNUAL AMOUNT
Weekly paycheck	$	x 52	$
Biweekly paycheck	$	x 26	$
Semimonthly paycheck	$	x 24	$
Monthly paycheck	$	x 12	$
Alimony	$	x 12	$
Child support	$	x 12	$
Disability check	$	x 12	$
Rental income	$	x 12	$
Quarterly payment	$	x 4	$
Semiannual payment	$	x 2	$
Annual payment	$	x 1	$
TOTAL	$		$

Now that you have your annual income total, you're ready to figure out how you spend that money.

TRACKING YOUR EXPENSES

Most people can count the number of their income sources on one hand—but that's certainly not the case with expenditures. There are an infinite number of ways you can spend your money.

Luckily, in our modern world of online banking and debit and credit cards, this kind of tracking is not nearly as labor-intensive as it might sound. Log onto your bank and credit card website (or gather together your bank and credit card statements, as well as your check register, if you have stuck with the paper-based system), and use the information to fill out Worksheet 2–2. Once you have completed that worksheet, you'll have an idea of your spending habits, and we can hone your understanding of where your money goes. If you're new to budgeting, this might feel a little odd, since some of your expenditures are going to be irregular, such as the car repair you did last spring, your spouse's dental surgery, or the amount you spent on a vacation. That's okay. When you create your budget, use the information you gather from over the last year to get an idea of what a typical year of expenditures looks like. It helps you build room in your budget for your irregular expenditures.

WORKSHEET 2–2:
Tracking Your Expenditures

WEEKLY SPENDING	AMOUNT	MULTIPLY BY	ANNUAL AMOUNT
Groceries and household items (includes toiletries and cleaning supplies)	$	× 52	$
Entertainment	$	× 52	$
Dining out, including coffee and lunch	$	× 52	$
Laundry/dry cleaning	$	× 52	$
Gas/tolls/parking	$	× 52	$
Public transportation	$	× 52	$
Church/charitable contributions	$	× 52	$
Postage and office supplies	$	× 52	$
Walk-around money (include whatever cash you regularly carry for random weekly expenses)	$	× 52	$

MONTHLY SPENDING	AMOUNT	MULTIPLY BY	ANNUAL AMOUNT
Mortgage/rent	$	× 12	$
Car payment/lease	$	× 12	$
Electric bill (average)	$	× 12	$
Gas bill (average)	$	× 12	$
Water bill	$	× 12	$
Sewer bill	$	× 12	$
Trash pickup bill	$	× 12	$
Cable/Internet/satellite bill	$	× 12	$
Telephone bill	$	× 12	$
Cell phone bill	$	× 12	$
Bank charges (maintenance and debit card fees)	$	× 12	$
Personal care (haircuts, manicures, etc.)	$	× 12	$
Home equity loan	$	× 12	$
Other loans	$	× 12	$
Credit card bill (if you have more than one, total all payments together here)	$	× 12	$
Child support	$	× 12	$
Alimony	$	× 12	$
Clothing	$	× 12	$
Medical expenses (include copays and prescriptions)	$	× 12	$
Memberships (gyms, professional organizations, religious institutions, etc.)	$	× 12	$

QUARTERLY EXPENSES	AMOUNT	MULTIPLY BY	ANNUAL AMOUNT
Car maintenance	$	× 4	$
Home maintenance	$	× 4	$
Tuition (if you pay your child's college tuition more or less often than quarterly, simply multiply the amount of your payment by the number of payments you make in a year)	$	× 4	$
Nonholiday gifts (include birthday, wedding, and baby gifts)	$	× 4	$
SEMIANNUAL EXPENSES	**AMOUNT**	**MULTIPLY BY**	**ANNUAL AMOUNT**
Auto insurance	$	× 2	$
Property taxes	$	× 2	$
ANNUAL EXPENSES	**AMOUNT**	**MULTIPLY BY**	**ANNUAL AMOUNT**
Homeowner's or renter's insurance	$	× 1	$
Vehicle registration and excise tax	$	× 1	$
Car repair	$	× 1	$
Home repair	$	× 1	$
Holiday gifts	$	× 1	$
Vacation	$	× 1	$
OTHER EXPENSES	**AMOUNT**	**MULTIPLY BY**	**ANNUAL AMOUNT**
	$	×	$
	$	×	$
	$	×	$
TOTAL	$		$

The total expenditures you come up with should be lower than the total income figure you came up with in Worksheet 2–1. If you are either spending every penny that comes in or spending more than you make, then you will need to find some ways to reduce your expenditures. Even if you are already spending less than you earn, you should ask if there's enough left over at the end of each month for you to beef up your retirement savings. If not, then it's time to start looking at your expenditures and figure out what you can cut.

This may seem overwhelming at first, especially if you are new to budgeting. You may feel as if there's nothing you can cut without sacrificing your quality of life. But the wonderful thing about creating a budget is that it is specific, personal, and subjective. A budget is not there to tell you what you cannot have—instead, it is a road map you create to direct your path to the things you desire. Determining what you want most can help you figure out where you can cut expenses without damaging the lifestyle you love.

An important way to categorize and rank the priorities in your budget is to separate your needs from your wants, and then rank them both. That way, you can find places to cut expenses without sacrificing your priorities. Worksheet 2–3: Needs and Wants Analysis can help.

Needs versus Wants

We all have a set of needs: a place to live, utilities, food, clothing, and transportation. Within them are nuances of importance, influenced by our wants and other needs. For instance, both a self-employed person and a CEO of a corporation need clothes. However, what each of them needs their clothing to do can be vastly different. If the work-at-homer loves fashion, she might still have a large clothing budget and splurge on big-name designers because looking good is an important want in her life. That is all right, as long as she budgets for her clothing needs and wants accordingly.

Similarly, the needs of a young twenty-something just starting out in his career will be different from the needs of someone who hopes to retire in five years.

Saving for retirement is a priority for you, so you may be able to forgo some of the things you have always seen as needs. Previously, you might have felt that maintaining a membership at a local golf course or country club was necessary for making and keeping business contacts.

As you get closer to retirement, you may now find that cutting that expense will help your retirement savings.

Wherever you have a choice in your needs or wants expenditures, find a less expensive option. In order to prioritize your expenses in such a way, however, you will need to figure out exactly what you care about most. That's what Worksheet 2–3 is for.

WORKSHEET 2-3:
Needs and Wants Analysis

NEED	YEARLY COST	IMPORTANCE (1 is least important; 5 is most important)				
Groceries/household items	$	1	2	3	4	5
Laundry/dry cleaning	$	1	2	3	4	5
Gas/tolls/parking	$	1	2	3	4	5
Postage and office supplies	$	1	2	3	4	5
Mortgage/rent	$	1	2	3	4	5
Car payment/lease/public transportation	$	1	2	3	4	5
Electric bill	$	1	2	3	4	5
Gas bill	$	1	2	3	4	5
Water bill	$	1	2	3	4	5
Sewer bill	$	1	2	3	4	5
Trash pickup bill	$	1	2	3	4	5
Cable/Internet/satellite bill	$	1	2	3	4	5
Telephone bill	$	1	2	3	4	5
Cell phone bill	$	1	2	3	4	5
Personal care	$	1	2	3	4	5
Clothing	$	1	2	3	4	5
	$	1	2	3	4	5
	$	1	2	3	4	5
	$	1	2	3	4	5

WANT	YEARLY COST	IMPORTANCE (1 is least important; 5 is most important)				
Entertainment	$	1	2	3	4	5
Dining out	$	1	2	3	4	5
Church/charitable contributions	$	1	2	3	4	5
Memberships	$	1	2	3	4	5
Nonholiday gifts	$	1	2	3	4	5
Holiday gifts	$	1	2	3	4	5
Vacation	$	1	2	3	4	5
	$	1	2	3	4	5
	$	1	2	3	4	5
	$	1	2	3	4	5

Now that you have thought about your ranking for your various needs and wants, it's time to compare your rankings with your spending habits. This will help you determine if you're overspending on wants (or needs that you care less about). Once you understand where your spending does not reflect your priorities, it will be much easier to make cuts in your expenditures that will allow you to maximize your savings. With this examination of which needs and wants are most important to you, you can start focusing your spending on the things that are most important to you, and making cuts where appropriate.

Taking Another Look at Expenses

Just because you now know where to make your cuts doesn't mean you know exactly how to go about doing that. That's what Worksheet 2–4: Reworking Your Expenses is for. This worksheet will help you think about ways you can change your expenses and figure out how much money those changes will save you.

This worksheet includes some expenses that we did not rank in Worksheet 2–3. While you must pay back things such as loans and pay for medical care and home/auto repair and maintenance, you may be able to negotiate more favorable terms and prices in order to reduce your cost. In addition, you do not need to make changes to every expense—or even most of them. The point is to make the most judicious cuts possible so that you can find extra money in your budget for savings without affecting your priorities.

Though this is all presented to you in a single neat table, this is by no means a quick process. It can take some time to implement your plans for lowering your expenses, so feel free to work on your action plan (your "Ways to Reduce") over the span of several weeks, or even months, if it involves major shifts (like selling a house or a car). Even if your ways to reduce expenses are more modest, it's okay to pace yourself on the negotiations, contract changes, and other methods that require more than just a change of habit on your part. The most important thing is that you know what your expenses are and have a plan in place to reduce them.

WORKSHEET 2-4:
Reworking Your Expenses

EXPENSE	CURRENT AMOUNT	WAYS TO REDUCE	NEW AMOUNT
Groceries/ household items	$		$
Entertainment	$		$
Dining out	$		$
Laundry/dry cleaning	$		$
Gas/tolls/parking	$		$
Public transportation	$		$
Church/charitable contributions	$		$
Postage and office supplies	$		$
Walk-around money	$		$

EXPENSE	CURRENT AMOUNT	WAYS TO REDUCE	NEW AMOUNT
Mortgage/rent	$		$
Car payment/ lease	$		$
Electric bill	$		$
Gas bill	$		$
Water bill	$		$
Sewer bill	$		$
Trash pickup bill	$		$
Cable/Internet/ satellite bill	$		$
Telephone bill	$		$
Cell phone bill	$		$
Bank charges	$		$
Personal care	$		$
Home equity loan	$		$
Other loans	$		$
Credit card bill	$		$
Clothing	$		$
Medical expenses	$		$

EXPENSE	CURRENT AMOUNT	WAYS TO REDUCE	NEW AMOUNT
Memberships	$		$
Car maintenance	$		$
Home maintenance	$		$
Tuition	$		$
Nonholiday gifts	$		$
Auto insurance	$		$
Property taxes	$		$
Homeowner's/renter's insurance	$		$
Vehicle registration	$		$
Car repair	$		$
Home repair	$		$
Holiday gifts	$		$
Vacation	$		$
Total expenses that cannot change (includes child support and alimony)	$		$
TOTAL	$		$

Balancing Your Budget

Now that you have an idea of your income, your expenses, and ways to reduce those expenses, it's time to see how much room in your budget you have created in order to maximize your retirement savings. This is one of the simplest parts of creating your budget—you just need to subtract.

WORKSHEET 2-5:

Is Your Budget Balanced?

Income	$
Expenses	– $
Balance	= $

If your balance is either a negative number or not as large as you'd like it to be, it's time to head back to Worksheet 2–4 and find some more ways to cut your expenses. You may also want to look into ways to increase your income if you feel you've done all the cutting you can do.

Remember that a budget is a living document. This is not something you can do once and then forget about. You need to consistently return to your budget to revise it as your life changes—whether those changes are to your income, your expenditures, or your circumstances.

Consistently adjusting and tweaking your budget means that you are always working toward the life goals that are most important to you, rather than letting your financial life go on autopilot. Taking the time to review your budget on a regular basis (about every three months is good) means you get to frequently check on how your goals are progressing, which can be awfully exciting.

DIGITAL BUDGETING OPTIONS

If the thought of budgeting is only unpleasant to you because you can't stand the thought of tracking your finances by hand, not to worry. There are plenty of products and services out there that can take the pain out of tracking expenses. Here is a short list of budgeting programs (including desktop software, online options, and mobile apps) that are an alternative to paper and pencil budgeting:

1. Mint (https://mint.intuit.com)—This free online-only budgeting software program by Intuit is simple to use and easy to set up. You securely link the program with your various bank accounts and credit cards, and the site will automatically track and categorize your spending. With smartphone and mobile apps available, Mint allows you to check on your finances anytime and anywhere. It also will allow you to track investments and set savings goals, if you would like a one-stop shop for your budgeting needs.

2. Quicken (www.quicken.com)—If the idea of providing Mint (or any other online tool) with your account information makes you uncomfortable, Quicken, which is another product by Intuit, might be a better choice for you. It is one of the oldest and most popular personal finance software programs available. With it, you can also track and categorize your expenses, as well as sync your accounts through your computer to the software. The setup is simple, and the newest version of the software includes smartphone and mobile apps, which will allow you to handle finances anywhere. The biggest downside to Quicken is that older versions are "retired" after a certain amount of time. At that point, the online features and formatted files for the retired version no longer work, which means you are forced to purchase the updated version, and often learn a new interface that comes with that upgrade.

3. BudgetPulse (www.budgetpulse.com)—This website provides no-frills budgeting software for free. It does not sync with your bank accounts, which means you have no potential security concerns—but you will have to manually enter your information or upload it from a Quicken or Microsoft Excel file. This is a good option for those who are concerned about security and are willing to be a little more hands-on in their electronic budgeting.

4. YNAB (www.youneedabudget.com)—You Need a Budget (YNAB for short) is an online budgeting program based on the envelope method, wherein budgeters set money aside for specific categories of spending. The program guides you through the process of budgeting, setting goals and sticking to them, and reconciling accounts through manual and automatic tracking. YNAB is geared toward teaching users how to budget and make managing their finances a

habit, and it offers an easy-to-use app as well as access to financial literacy classes, tutorials, a community of YNAB users, blog posts, and budgeting tools and tricks. YNAB costs $84 per year, but you can try the program free for thirty-four days.

5. Marcus Insights (www.marcus.com/us/en/insights)—Marcus Insights is a free mobile app associated with the bank Marcus by Goldman Sachs, but users do not have to be Marcus customers to download and use the app. When you download the app to your Android or Apple device and sync it with your financial accounts, the program analyzes your financial data to give you an at-a-glance visualization of your cash flow. The app also provides you with a daily summary of your spending, which includes automatic categorization of your purchases.

6. Personal Capital (www.personalcapital.com)—As an account aggregator, Personal Capital allows you to track and understand every single penny in all of your financial accounts. Once you link up all of your various accounts, including your bank accounts, investments, mortgage, credit cards, and any other accounts, Personal Capital summarizes your finances and offers you basic investment guidance. The interface, which you can use on the mobile app or on your desktop, gives you an understanding of all of your spending and account balances, and allows you to categorize your spending by date, merchant, and type of expense. The program also offers a retirement planner tool that can help you build, manage, and forecast your retirement savings.

MORE BUDGETING SOFTWARE OPTIONS

The programs mentioned here are the tip of the iceberg of budgeting software options, and there is likely a program that will work for even the most budget-phobic. For reviews of more software options, check out *The Balance*'s 2021 best-of list at www.thebalance.com/best-personal-finance-software-4171938.

CHAPTER 2 TAKEAWAYS

☑ In the five years before your retirement, you should focus on two financial priorities: saving for retirement and paying off your consumer debt.

☑ To maximize your money, plan on prioritizing your saving and debt payoff in the following order:

1. Save up to the employer match in your defined contribution plan
2. Eliminate consumer debt
3. Max out your IRA
4. Max out your defined contribution plan

☑ Creating a budget while you are still working will allow you to get used to tracking your income and expenses and can help you find more money to send toward your retirement.

☑ Once you have determined what your regular and irregular expenses are, you can begin finding ways to reduce the expenses that do not align with your goals and preferences.

☑ Budgeting with software, an online program, or a mobile app can be much less labor-intensive than traditional methods.

What to Do When

YEARS TO RETIREMENT	WHAT TO DO
Five	Gather your financial information and complete Worksheets 2–1 through 2–5 to find ways to increase your savings.
Five	Implement an action plan for reducing your expenses.
Four through one	At least once a year, reassess your pre-retirement budget and make any necessary changes.
Four through one	Work to pay off consumer debt. As you pay it off, send the "payment" to your retirement savings.

CHAPTER 3

Income in Retirement

In this chapter, you'll learn the two main strategies for income withdrawal in retirement: the 4 percent withdrawal rule and the bucket method. You will also understand how federal regulations govern your required minimum distributions from your tax-deferred retirement accounts once you have reached age seventy-two. Finally, you'll learn what to expect from annuities if you would prefer a more hands-off approach to accessing your retirement income.

Savings versus Income

One of the reasons retirement planning can seem so confusing, particularly for those within a few years of retirement, is that for the majority of your career, you focused on the savings/accumulation aspect of retirement planning. When you are in your thirties (or even your fifties), most of the advice you hear is about amping up your savings and building your nest egg. It's not until close to the end of your career that it might occur to you to ask, "Okay, so what do I do with this big old stack of cash?" While everyone can benefit from saving more, only those close to retirement need to know the intricacies of making their money last through thirty or more years of withdrawals.

Thankfully, your money is not going to be dwindling away through your retirement years. You will continue to invest the remaining money so that it can keep working for you throughout the years. The fact that your money will continue to grow in retirement is the reason why determining how much you can afford to withdraw each year is more complicated than simply dividing your nest egg by the number of years you hope to live. Your money should continue to earn interest so that you slow the drawdown on the assets and you don't have to worry about outliving your money.

There are two primary strategies for fund withdrawal in retirement: the 4 percent rule and the bucket method. Each one has its benefits, and the two strategies can be used in conjunction. In addition, we'll look at the required minimum distributions (RMDs) for IRAs and 401(k) accounts in order to determine how those RMDs will affect your retirement withdrawal strategy. We'll finish up with a look at annuities.

The 4 Percent Withdrawal Rule

This retirement withdrawal rule of thumb is officially known as systematic withdrawal. The 4 percent aspect of this style of withdrawal was proposed by financial adviser William Bengen in 1994.

BENGEN'S TWENTY-FIVE-YEAR-OLD PREDICTIONS

You can read Bengen's 1994 study, "Determining Withdrawal Rates Using Historical Data," at www.retailinvestor.org/pdf/Bengen1.pdf. In the study, Bengen uses a fictional example of how the market might fluctuate between 2004 and 2009 in order to help his readers understand why previous withdrawal strategies might not work during a downturn. His hypothetical example is interesting to read, as it was a reasonably accurate prediction. Although he was off by a single year, Bengen accidentally predicted our economic downturn of 2007/2008.

Bengen used historical market data in order to determine a safe drawdown rate in retirement that would allow an investor's money to comfortably last for the rest of his life. Bengen's study demonstrated that if a retiree were to withdraw 4 percent of her assets in the first year and increase that withdrawal by a small amount each year to account for inflation, then the savings would last for thirty years.

For example, let's say you retire with $1 million in retirement savings. During your first year of retirement, you would plan on withdrawing 4 percent of your savings, or $40,000, as retirement income. The next year, you would increase your withdrawal amount slightly, taking an additional 3 percent of the $40,000 (or $1,200) in order to cover inflation. Each year, you would continue this inflation adjustment, to keep the same buying power for each year of your retirement.

The 4 percent withdrawal rule still has plenty of fans. Considering the fact that the historical rate of return on stocks generally hovers at around 10 percent, withdrawing 4 percent per year (plus inflation) seemed, for many years, to be a no-brainer method of staying ahead of your withdrawal rate. Unfortunately, the 4 percent rule serves retirees well in good economic times, but not necessarily in bad. Any retirees who were committed to this strategy learned the hard way in 2008 and 2020 that systematic withdrawal can bite you if the market takes a downturn.

INFLATION CALCULATOR

If you would like to calculate how much a dollar's value has changed over the years, the Bureau of Labor Statistics offers an inflation calculator that uses the average Consumer Price Index for a given year (www.bls.gov/data/inflation_calculator.htm). While no calculator can read the future and tell you exactly how inflation will affect your retirement income, seeing just how much less a dollar buys today when compared to twenty or thirty years ago can help you plan for inflation in retirement.

UNDERSTANDING HOW MARKET DOWNTURNS CAN AFFECT SYSTEMATIC WITHDRAWAL

During the years you were investing money in your portfolio, you may have used dollar-cost averaging in order to maximize your profits. With this strategy, you invest an equal amount of money regularly into a portfolio. Since the market fluctuates, sometimes your regular investment will buy more shares, because each share has gone down in value, and sometimes the investment will buy fewer shares, because each share costs more. This works out to the investor's advantage because the practice lowers the average cost per share over time, which will maximize profits. You own more low-price shares that can go up, and you own fewer high-price shares that can go down.

Unfortunately, when you are using the systematic withdrawal strategy, you are vulnerable to what David Babbel, professor emeritus of business economics and public policy at the Wharton School of the University of Pennsylvania, calls "reverse dollar-cost averaging." This means that when the market is down, you will have to sell more shares in order to withdraw the same amount of money. That means you have fewer shares left to bounce back when the price goes up again later.

This is why a strict adherence to the 4 percent rule can be a dicey withdrawal strategy. It's better to regard this rule as a rule of thumb— especially since this conventional wisdom does not take into account your asset allocation. (That is, how exactly you have your money invested.) Depending on how conservative or aggressive your portfolio is, the 4 percent rule may itself be too aggressive or conservative a withdrawal strategy.

It's important to remember that the 4 percent rule is based on a fairly passive investment strategy: buy-and-hold. This strategy is based on the (historically accurate) view that the market tends to go up over time, despite periods of decline or volatility. Using a buy-and-hold strategy throughout your career, while you have time to allow your investments to recover from downturns, is a sound method for building your retirement nest egg. However, simply holding your investments during your retirement can do a number on your portfolio, especially if you happen to retire during a market downturn. Instead, it's a good idea to pair the 4 percent drawdown strategy with strategic asset allocation (also known as the bucket method) in order to be sure that your money lasts your entire life.

WHY CHOOSE THE 4 PERCENT METHOD?

The potential risks of systematic withdrawal may make it seem like a poor withdrawal strategy, particularly if you are feeling gun-shy after seeing the market's 2020 roller coaster ride. However, the 4 percent method still has a place in a savvy retiree's withdrawal strategies, as long as you enter into it with your eyes wide open:

- The 4 percent method can be helpful for those retirees lucky enough to also have a pension, as it provides a simple method for dealing with non-pension retirement savings.

- Using systematic withdrawal in conjunction with the bucket method outlined later in this chapter can help you take advantage of the simplicity of the 4 percent rule while also building a cushion against potential market volatility.

- If you are willing to pare down your withdrawal rate to 3.5 percent or even 3 percent, systematic withdrawal can give you a similar sense of security that the 4 percent rule has promised for the past twenty-five years.

Using this strategy with caution, rather than regarding it as a set-in-stone rule, can help you to enjoy your retirement income comfortably for the rest of your life.

Using the 4 Percent Method for Withdrawal

PROS	CONS
Simple to understand and act on.	Still requires regular check-ins on your investments to ensure your nest egg's security.
Historically, 4 percent provides a safe withdrawal rate.	Past performance does not guarantee future results. A safe withdrawal rate in 2019 is not necessarily a safe rate in 2029. Or 2039.
Accounts for 3 percent inflation per year.	Periods of high inflation can hurt your buying power. That means you might be faced with the choice of lowering your standard of living or withdrawing more money from your accounts.
Systematic withdrawal can be reduced to 3.5 or 3 percent to ensure your money's longevity.	It could be difficult to live on 4 percent per year, let alone 3.5 or 3 percent.

THE BUCKET METHOD FOR WITHDRAWAL

The bucket method of retirement income withdrawal starts with the assumption that retirees will have to ride out some market volatility during their golden years. Since it's foolhardy to assume that all thirty (or more) years of your retirement will see market gains, the bucket method is a savvy way to prepare for the times when your portfolio takes a hit. In order to account for potential market volatility, investors using the bucket method split their portfolios into separate income "buckets," each of which will be intended to handle a different time period in retirement. The most common way to allocate buckets is to separate them into three asset classes and time periods:

1. **YEARS 1-5.** Your first bucket is intended to take care of your finances in the first five years of retirement. Since you want both stability and liquidity in this time period, the money in this bucket will be placed in cash equivalent assets, where you know the principal is protected. Cash equivalents include CDs, US Treasury bills, and money market funds. Having the money in this bucket will provide you with the stability you need to know that your principal (and income) for the next five years is protected, while still giving the remainder of your money in the other two buckets the time it needs to continue to grow.

2. **YEARS 6-15.** The second bucket will take care of your retirement income during the middle portion of your retirement—about year six through year fifteen. Since you will not be tapping this money until you have gotten a few years into your retirement, you can afford to be a little more aggressive with your investments. For most retirees, the second bucket will consist of a mix of bonds and stocks, leaning more toward the safety of bonds. While you do have the time to ride out market fluctuations with this bucket, you want to ensure that your money will be there once you reach this time period. The goal of this bucket is to allocate your assets in such a way that will reasonably protect the principal and provide the opportunity to grow.

3. **YEARS 16 AND FURTHER.** The third bucket is where you will be most aggressive in your investments, because you will not be accessing the money in this portion of your portfolio until after you have been retired about fifteen years. Here, you can afford to invest in high-risk/high-return assets, such as stocks and other types of equities. With additional time on your side, you can both ride out the volatility of the market and reap the potential benefits.

DEFINING STOCKS AND BONDS

A stock represents ownership (also known as equity) in a company. Investors purchase stocks with the expectation that their value will change, either by going up or down. The goal of stock purchases is to buy low and sell high, although some stocks offer dividends as well. Stocks are by definition a potentially risky (and potentially lucrative) investment. A bond, on the other hand, represents a company's debt. By purchasing a bond, an investor has in effect loaned money to the company in exchange for interest payments and a promise of repayment at a future date, known as the maturity date. Bonds are generally more conservative investments.

As the years go by, retirees using the bucket method will need to redistribute their assets from one bucket to another in order to continue to meet each portion's goals. For instance, as you use up the funds in your first bucket, you will need to move some of the second bucket's funds into the first bucket, and move some of the third bucket's funds into the second. While these redistributions might not always be necessary—for instance, if the market is doing well and your returns are such that each bucket has maintained or exceeded your goals—you will have to keep a regular eye on how your three-part portfolio is doing.

The more structured nature of the bucket withdrawal strategy can be both a benefit and a drawback. Since each bucket will have certain goals tied to it, the strategy can help to ensure you remain disciplined in your withdrawals and spending. In addition, breaking the overwhelming task of allocating assets for retirement into three smaller goals can relieve a great deal of stress.

Using this retirement withdrawal strategy can also potentially help make retirement possible for those who have not saved as much as they might like. Since you are investing a portion of your money for the long term, you could theoretically end your career before you've reached your ideal nest egg amount. However, it is important to remember that there are no guarantees—so even if you are willing to let compound interest do its magic on your third bucket of investments, always hedge your bets. You can do so by delaying Social Security benefits (more on that in Chapter 5) and by waiting until the maximum age to access some of your tax-deferred accounts (explained in detail in the next part of this chapter).

Since the bucket method requires hands-on maintenance, it may not work well for a retiree with a "set-it-and-forget-it" mindset. If the idea of keeping careful track of your investments sounds about as much fun as cleaning the local football stadium with your toothbrush, you may either want to partner with a trusted financial adviser to help you make those decisions, or you may want to look into other methods of handling your retirement income. We'll look at annuities in particular later in this chapter.

Using the Bucket Method for Withdrawal

PROS	CONS
Designed to ride out market volatility.	Requires hands-on maintenance, which may be overwhelming to some retirees.
Forces retirees to be disciplined and follow a budget.	Undisciplined retirees may have trouble following their bucket method.
Provides an opportunity for further asset growth in retirement, meaning individuals with smaller nest eggs may still be able to retire on time.	As with any investments, there are no guarantees of returns.
Can be customized to each retiree's needs and goals.	Can be somewhat difficult for the layperson to understand and implement.

Your withdrawal strategy will probably be affected by the IRS rules regarding required minimum distributions (RMDs) for 401(k) and IRA accounts. Whether you decide on a 4 percent withdrawal strategy or a bucket strategy, or a combination of the two, you will likely have some decisions made for you by the IRS. Later in this chapter, we'll discuss how required minimum distributions affect withdrawal strategies.

TARGET DATE FUNDS: POTENTIALLY THE BEST OF BOTH WORLDS

For savers who want an investment and withdrawal strategy that accounts for market volatility but still allows for a set-it-and-forget-it attitude, target date funds can be a good fit. These mutual funds, which are generally found within your 401(k) or IRA investment options, offer you a single fund that is professionally managed and diversified based upon your target retirement date. That means your asset allocation (the amount of money you have invested in stocks versus bonds) gradually becomes more conservative as you get nearer to retirement. For instance, a fifty-year-old in 2021 with a fund target dated for retirement in 2036 will have more of her investments placed in higher-risk/high-return assets right now, but that asset allocation will gradually shift to lower-risk/higher-stability assets as she gets closer to her retirement.

Target date funds have been around since the early 1990s, but they have become much more popular in the past fifteen years for two major reasons. First, the 2006 US legislation that allowed for employers to auto-enroll their employees in defined contribution retirement plans created a need for a default plan that would provide appropriate asset allocation and rebalancing even if unreviewed over time. Target date funds were a perfect fit for this need. In addition, the 2008 financial downturn was disastrous for any new retirees who had not rebalanced their portfolios to be more conservative as they approached retirement. Target date funds offer an attractive alternative to manually rebalancing your asset allocation as you approach retirement.

Target Date Funds and the Glide Path

While target date funds do offer an easy "default" setting to help prepare your money for retirement, you should still make sure you understand your fund's glide path. The glide path is the term for the fund's investment strategy leading up to and past your target retirement date. The glide path describes how the asset allocation becomes more conservative over time. Some target date funds have a glide path that becomes static as of your target retirement date, meaning your money is no longer invested in any potentially higher-risk/high-return assets as of your retirement date. Since you are theoretically going to be retired for several decades, such a conservative glide path may not be optimal for your needs.

If you are invested in a target date fund, it may make sense to either invest in one with a target date just a few years after your projected actual retirement, find one with a glide path that continues to invest after your retirement date, or have a separate investment for long-term growth outside of the target date fund.

Required Minimum Distributions

When you put money in tax-deferred accounts such as a 401(k) or an IRA, you are putting off paying taxes on that money until you withdraw it. That's a boon to workers who are attempting to lower their tax burden during their career and who are focused on growing their money as inexpensively as possible.

However, having money in a tax-deferred account does mean you will have to pay Uncle Sam your share eventually. We'll talk in much more detail in Chapter 6 about the tax implications of accessing your IRA and 401(k) accounts in retirement. For now, let's focus on how the IRS requires you to access your money.

The IRS needs individuals with tax-deferred accounts to actually withdraw money (and thereby pay taxes), rather than keep the money in those accounts indefinitely. Because of this, the IRS requires each account holder to begin withdrawing money during the year that he reaches age seventy-two. There is a minimum amount you must withdraw, and you face a stiff penalty for failing to do so—the IRS will take 50 percent of the amount that should have been withdrawn.

The buck stops with you when it comes to calculating and withdrawing the correct RMD each year. Even if the custodian of your IRA or 401(k) does the math and paperwork for you, you are ultimately the responsible party. If you catch and correct an error prior to December 31 of the distribution year, you can avoid facing the penalty, but once the year has passed, you are on the hook. (The IRS recognizes that sometimes mistakes do happen. If you take less than the required amount because of a reasonable error, and if you take the appropriate steps to fix the error, you may be able to apply for a waiver of the penalty.) Figuring out your RMD takes some calculation and will require three pieces of information:

1. Your date of birth.

2. The balance of each tax-deferred account as of December 31 of the previous year.

3. The correct IRS distribution table. These tables can be found in Appendix B of IRS Publication 590 (www.irs.gov/publications/p590b#en_US_2019_publink1000231236). These tables calculate life expectancy based upon your age and therefore give you a number (corresponding to the number of years they expect you to live), by which you will divide your balance in order to determine your RMD.

There are three different IRS distribution tables:

1. **TABLE I**—Single Life Expectancy is the distribution table for those individuals who have inherited a tax-deferred account from the owner. That means if your father made you the beneficiary of his IRA, when he dies, you will use Table I to determine your RMD from that IRA each year.

2. **TABLE II**—Joint Life and Last Survivor Expectancy is for calculating RMDs for an IRA owner whose spouse is more than ten years younger and is the sole beneficiary of the IRA. If you are in a May–December marriage, this is the table you will use to determine your RMD.

3. **TABLE III**—Uniform Lifetime is the one the vast majority of IRA owners will use.

Let's assume you were born on February 4, 1950, and will therefore blow out seventy-two birthday candles in 2022. In order to determine your RMD for 2022, you will need to find out the balance of your tax-deferred accounts as of December 31, 2021. The rules stipulate that you can figure out your RMDs for all of your IRAs and take that amount out from any one IRA or from whatever combination of IRAs that floats your boat. But if you also have multiple 401(k) accounts, you will need to take the specific RMD out from each one of them. You are not allowed to lump those RMDs together like you can for your IRAs.

Let's say you only have one IRA, which had a balance of $250,000 at the end of 2021. To calculate your RMD, you look up your age on Table III and divide your balance by the distribution period determined by your age—in this case 25.6. That means you must take out at least $9,766 in 2022 ($250,000 / 25.6 = $9,765.63, rounded up to $9,766).

THE OPERATIVE WORD IS "MINIMUM"

It's important to remember that your required minimum distribution is just that: the minimum amount that you must take out of your account. You are welcome to withdraw more of your money if you so choose.

Of course, since your balance changes from year to year, reflecting both your withdrawals and the growth of your money, you will have to recalculate your RMD each year using your new end-of-year balance from the previous year and your new distribution period according to the IRS table.

REQUIRED BEGINNING DATE

Prior to the passage of the Setting Every Community Up for Retirement Enhancement (SECURE) Act in December 2019, the age for required minimum distributions was set at seventy-and-a-half. The determination of when you reached seventy-and-a-half was somewhat confusing (since your official date depended on whether you had a birthday in the first or second half of the year), which made for some difficult-to-parse rules about your required beginning date.

Now that the official RMD age is seventy-two, all tax-deferred account holders have the same required beginning date: You are required to take your first RMD by April 1 of the year following your seventy-second birthday. After that first RMD, however, you will be required to take each subsequent RMD by December 31.

That means the person with the February birthday can wait to take his first RMD until April 1, 2023, at which point he would calculate that RMD based on the age of seventy-two and his account balance as of December 31, 2021. However, he will also have to take his 2023 RMD in 2023, prior to the end of that year, based on his age of seventy-three and his account balance as of December 31, 2022.

Note that RMDs come into play only once you have reached seventy-two. You are allowed to withdraw any amount you like from your IRA and 401(k) accounts when you are between the ages of fifty-nine-and-a-half (the earliest you can take a penalty-free withdrawal from these tax-deferred accounts) and seventy-two.

Annuities

If everything you've read so far about withdrawal strategies has you convinced that it would be easier to just keep working and collecting a paycheck, don't worry. There are other alternatives out there that can allow you to focus on the fun part of retirement and worry less about money management.

In particular, if you would prefer to continue receiving the equivalent of a paycheck rather than manage your money, an annuity might be a good fit for you.

Annuities are a thriving part of the insurance industry, and they offer a type of structure and peace of mind that can't be found with other retirement income strategies. Of course, annuities also have their downsides, but for some retirees, they will be the right choice.

NOT ALL ANNUITIES ARE CREATED EQUAL

In this section, we'll discuss the most common types of annuities, including immediate and deferred annuities, which also happen to be the types that are easiest to understand. If you are interested in some of the more exotic products, such as equity-indexed and variable annuities, you can find excellent explanations of each of these products in *The AARP Retirement Survival Guide* by Julie Jason and in the expanded and updated edition of *Smart Women Finish Rich* by David Bach.

An annuity is a product sold by an insurance company. You pay the insurance company a lump sum, and the company will make regular, guaranteed payments to you, generally for the rest of your life. The insurance company uses your lump sum to make investments, thereby taking on the risks (and benefits) of investing. The company assumes it will make more money from investing your lump sum than it will have to pay out in your guaranteed payments.

While this might sound like an absolutely great deal for nervous investors, there are a couple of caveats that are important to remember. First, you cannot back out of an annuity. While most annuities will offer a short time period during which you can cancel a new policy, once you have reached the end of your cancellation period (also known as a "free look period"), you cannot get your lump sum back.

In addition, it's important to remember that insurance companies are not backed by the Federal Deposit Insurance Corporation (FDIC), which means your money is not guaranteed should your insurance carrier fail. This is why several rating agencies, such as Moody's Investors Service (www.moodys.com), offer metrics for determining the financial strength of insurance companies. Moody's rates companies from Aaa (exceptional financial security) through C (poor financial security). It makes sense to only look at annuities from insurance companies rated Aaa, Aa, or A.

IMMEDIATE ANNUITIES

These products may also be known as fixed immediate annuities, single premium immediate annuities, and income annuities. Purchasing one of these products will immediately provide you with a guaranteed retirement income for life. Since these products are immediate—that is, you hand over a lump sum now and start getting monthly (or quarterly or annual) checks as quickly as next month—they will generally cost more than deferred annuities, which build in some time for your initial payment to grow.

While some immediate annuities offer inflation offset features, which increase your monthly payments over the years in order to keep up with inflation, most bare-bones versions of these products only promise a guaranteed dollar amount each month. In addition, while most annuities are lifelong, some immediate annuity products offer limited terms, from ten to fifty years. What that means is that you are guaranteed monthly checks for the length of the term, but if you outlive that term, you will receive nothing after it ends. Retirees may be tempted by such term annuities because they are generally cheaper, and they could be one way to create the first "bucket" of retirement planning and withdrawal while other funds continue to grow in the market.

Term annuities can also potentially ensure a legacy for your family. In general, annuities are for you alone, meaning if you pass away just a few years after purchasing your annuity, your heirs will receive nothing. However, you can purchase an annuity for life with a term that is "certain." For instance, if you purchase a life annuity with twenty years certain, and you pass away eight years later, your beneficiary will continue to receive the payments you would have gotten for the twelve-year period between your death and the end of the certain term.

The taxes you pay on an immediate annuity depend upon where the lump sum comes from. If you are purchasing your immediate annuity with money in a taxable account, then you will only be charged taxes on a portion of your monthly annuity checks—the portion that represents gains on your investments. If, however, you purchase the annuity with a lump sum from a tax-deferred account, such as an IRA or 401(k), each monthly check you receive from the annuity will be considered fully taxable as income. In either case, the insurance company holding your annuity will send you a 1099-R form each year delineating the taxable amount of your annuity income, which you report to the IRS.

DEFERRED FIXED ANNUITIES

In some ways, deferred fixed annuities are much like their immediate brethren. Just like immediate annuities, you pay a lump sum (generally) to an insurance company or brokerage in exchange for future payments. But instead of immediately receiving checks from the annuity, the money remains in the investment vehicle and is allowed to grow, tax-deferred. The big difference between immediate and deferred annuities is how you access your money. Deferred annuities will allow you to withdraw money when you need it in whatever amount you need—with some important caveats. These annuities have something called a surrender period, a time during which you cannot withdraw your money without having to pay hefty fees. The surrender period can be as long as seven to ten years, meaning you are stuck waiting for your money when you might need it. (It's important to note, however, that some deferred fixed annuities will allow withdrawals of up to 10 percent of the account value without any fees during the surrender period.)

Deferred annuities, like other investments, tend to be more attractive if you have plenty of time available to allow them to grow. For most deferred annuities, you will have the option of turning the product into an immediate annuity after a certain amount of time has passed, or you can continue to withdraw money from the annuity as you need it.

Deferred fixed annuities also offer tax-deferred growth on your money, which means you will not be required to pay taxes on any growth until you withdraw your money. At that point, you will pay ordinary income tax on the interest. However, it's important to remember that with this, as with all tax-deferred growth vehicles, you will owe the IRS a 10 percent tax penalty if you withdraw money before you're fifty-nine-and-a-half. Finally, if your money is in a deferred fixed annuity at the time of your death, the total account value of your annuity will be paid directly to your beneficiary. With immediate fixed annuities, your heirs will be left with nothing in the event of your death.

UNDERSTANDING ANNUITY PITFALLS

So far, with the exception of the tax concerns, annuities probably seem like a fairly straightforward product. However, the world of annuities can be extremely difficult to navigate. For instance, both immediate and deferred annuities can provide either fixed or variable interest rates. For immediate annuities, an offer of a fixed rate means that you will be guaranteed payments that equal a percentage of your initial stake. For example, if you have a guaranteed 5 percent return on your $500,000 immediate annuity, you can expect to receive payments of $25,000 per year for life. Unfortunately, that amount of money will be worth less and less each year due to inflation, and inflation protection riders tend to be expensive, or they offer lower guaranteed rates.

Deferred fixed annuities work similarly to the guaranteed rate on Certificates of Deposit (CDs). The insurance company will guarantee that your investment will earn a certain fixed rate of return. In many cases, the "fixed" rate is an introductory teaser rate to get you excited about the product. After a certain time—usually a year—the teaser rate will start readjusting yearly based on market conditions, although there is a guaranteed minimum rate. You may also find deferred annuities that will offer more modest fixed rates for longer periods, although all "fixed" rates will eventually become a rate that is readjusted yearly with a promise of a guaranteed minimum.

Because they are insurance products, annuities are sold either by insurance agents or financial advisers with insurance licenses. In either case, your adviser will be commission-based and will be highly motivated to get you to sign on the dotted line.

In addition, while immediate and deferred fixed annuities are fairly easy to understand and compare (although shopping around for the best product, even with the simplest annuities, can feel like comparing apples to oranges), the more exotic annuities like equity-indexed annuities and many types of variable annuities are more difficult to wrap your head around. Add in the fact that the exotic annuities generally offer salespeople much higher commissions, and you may find yourself scheduling a meeting to talk about a simple immediate annuity and find yourself sitting through a sales pitch for something much more complex.

According to many retirement and investment experts, however, the biggest concern with annuities is the opportunity cost. Once you have placed your money into an annuity, it is no longer available to you to otherwise invest or spend. Since there is no way to access your principal, it is, for all intents and purposes, gone. This can be particularly problematic if the economy hits a period of high inflation. The immediate fixed annuity holder will suffer in that case because his guaranteed income will buy far less than anticipated, and the deferred fixed annuity holder will suffer because her guaranteed rate will not keep pace with inflation.

HEY! THERE ARE ANNUITIES IN MY 401(K)!

In addition to raising the age requirement for RMDs, the SECURE Act of 2019 also included provisions meant to encourage more employers to offer annuities within their 401(k) programs. Specifically, the SECURE Act insulates employers from legal risk if the insurer providing the annuity were unable to pay the promised annuity income. As long as the insurer providing the annuity is in good standing with the state insurance department in the state where the insurer is based, then the employer offering the annuity within its 401(k) is protected from potential lawsuits should the insurer fail.

This standard is remarkably low and does not give investors any recourse should their employer make a less-than-ideal choice for annuities within the 401(k). Additionally, the SECURE Act does not require employers to offer low-cost annuities. Tread cautiously and make sure you commit to fully researching any annuity offered through your 401(k).

WHY CHOOSE AN ANNUITY?

All that said, an annuity can be the right choice for some individuals. In particular, those who struggle with money discipline can be well served by an annuity—particularly an immediate annuity. If you know that having a large sum of money available to you will be an invitation to spend without thinking about the consequences, you should consider an annuity, as it will force you to slow down and budget.

If you are risk-averse and will see every dip in the market as a potential disaster, an annuity can give you peace of mind. There's no need to chew your fingernails when you know that the insurance company has given you a guarantee of payment. Alternatively, if you find finances boring beyond belief and would rather spend your time with friends and family and pursuing your hobbies, an annuity can be a relief for you. You won't have to regularly review your investments and handle readjustments if you know for a fact that your annuity check is coming month after month.

If you're interested in an annuity, keep these four things in mind:

1. Never place your entire nest egg into an annuity. It's better to simply annuitize enough of your retirement savings to create the minimum income you will need.

2. Don't commit to the first pitch you hear. Take the time to understand every aspect of each sales pitch and end any meeting with an adviser, agent, or broker that begins to feel high-pressure.

3. Consider waiting a few years. If you wait to purchase an immediate annuity until you are a few years into your retirement, you will receive higher payments with the same principal. That's because the older you are when you sign up, the higher the annuity payments will be. In addition, if you like the idea of an annuity but are turned off by concerns about tying up your money, you could purchase a term immediate annuity now, and another one down the road, thereby maximizing what you can do with your money.

4. Check the insurer's rating. Don't bother with any insurance company with a lower ranking than A.

Using an Immediate Annuity for Retirement Income

PROS	CONS
Provides guaranteed income, safe from undisciplined spending.	Unless you purchase a certain term, your heirs will receive nothing.
Very low risk.	You cannot access your money if you change your mind.
Easy to understand and set up.	Sold on commission, and therefore requires very careful shopping around.
Requires no hands-on money maintenance or understanding of investments.	Additional riders add to the complexity and the difficulty of comparing products among different insurance companies.

Using a Deferred Annuity for Retirement Income

PROS	CONS
Guaranteed rate of return.	"Fixed" rate will likely be readjusted yearly, and even the guaranteed minimum rate will be less than you will see in other investment vehicles.
Tax-deferred growth.	Possibility of losing value due to inflation.
No limit on withdrawals (after the surrender period).	The surrender period will tie up your money for as much as seven years.
Can be turned into an immediate annuity for guaranteed income.	Account value of deferred fixed annuity is paid directly to your beneficiary at the time of your death.

Thinking about Mortality

Throughout this chapter, many of the recommendations are based on the assumption that you can expect to live a long and healthy life. However, that is not necessarily the case for every retiree. If your family has a history of heart disease, cancer, or other health threats, you may not need to be as cautious with your money as someone whose family members regularly make it to one hundred years old. While knowing you may have poor health after retirement can affect your health insurance decisions (which we'll discuss in Chapters 7 and 8), it can also affect your plans for your overall retirement.

Even if you have some troubling health trends throughout your family history, it's important to remember that the older you get, the better your life expectancy is. A baby born in 1956 had a life expectancy of about sixty-eight years, but an individual who turns sixty-five in 2021 has a life expectancy of eighty-four years. A seventy-five-year-old's life expectancy in 2021 is just under eighty-seven years.

While it is important to keep your mortality in mind while making your retirement withdrawal plans, don't forget that you have many reasons to be optimistic about your life expectancy.

CHAPTER 3 TAKEAWAYS

☑ With the 4 percent withdrawal rule (also known as systematic withdrawal), you will withdraw 4 percent of your savings each year in retirement, with annual adjustments for inflation. This strategy assumes that your portfolio will grow more than 4 percent each year. However, if you follow this strategy, a large market downturn could jeopardize your nest egg.

☑ The bucket method for retirement income assumes that you will have to ride out some market volatility during your retirement. To protect your investments, you place your money in three separate "buckets" corresponding to when you anticipate needing the money. Throughout your retirement, you will rebalance your money among the buckets to maintain both the stability and growth you need for your short- and long-term retirement income needs.

☑ Target date funds can offer a set-it-and-forget-it version of the bucket method, since these funds automatically shift from more aggressive to more conservative investments as you near retirement. However, make sure you understand the specific investment strategy both before and after your target retirement date.

☑ Tax-deferred accounts like 401(k) accounts and IRAs have required minimum distributions (RMDs) once you reach the age of seventy-two. You will calculate your RMD amount based upon your account balance of the previous year and the correct IRS distribution table.

☑ When you purchase an annuity from an insurer, you will receive regular, guaranteed payments. However, the money you pay into the annuity is tied up, meaning there is a big opportunity cost for these products. Though basic annuities are easy to understand, there are a number of exotic and complex annuity products, and insurance agents are often paid higher commissions for selling such products.

☑ When planning for your retirement income, it is better to assume you will live a long and healthy life, even if you have reason to worry about potential health conditions.

What to Do When

YEARS TO RETIREMENT	WHAT TO DO
Five	If you have enough liquid funds and plan to use a deferred fixed annuity, make your purchase now to give it time to grow before you reach retirement.
Five	Discuss with your financial adviser your planned withdrawal strategy.
Four through one	Meet with your financial adviser at least once a year to reassess your withdrawal strategy.
One	Purchase an immediate annuity this year if you plan to use one.

CHAPTER 4

Find the Right Financial Planner

WHAT YOU'LL LEARN IN THIS CHAPTER

Partnering with a financial professional to prepare for retirement can help relieve your stress about the big decisions ahead of you, but how do you find the right adviser for your needs? This chapter offers you a primer on the most common types of advisers you may encounter and the most common compensation models you can expect when you hire a financial planner. You will also learn what rules and regulations govern the various types of financial professionals. Finally, the chapter offers you several questions to ask when interviewing a potential adviser to help ensure you find a professional who will fit your needs.

There are many different types of financial planners and advisers, and only some of the titles that various financial advisers can use are regulated. Meeting someone who calls himself a financial planner could mean you've shaken hands with an insurance agent, a stockbroker, an investment adviser, a money coach, or a Certified Financial Planner (CFP).

If that's not confusing enough, different types of advisers are paid in different ways, which can seriously affect your bottom line. Even those with a good understanding of the financial world can be excused for feeling a little overwhelmed.

With all of this in mind, finding a trustworthy financial adviser can seem like an impossible task. But going it alone is not a good strategy for handling your retirement. Partnering with a financial adviser who is well versed in all of the rules, regulations, options, and opportunities facing you makes much more sense than trying to educate yourself from the ground up.

So how do you determine exactly whom to trust with your financial decisions? While the process of interviewing potential advisers might take some time and effort on your part, it is much less overwhelming than either finding you've placed your trust in someone you shouldn't have or trying to make all of your complex retirement decisions without any help. Let's take a moment to talk about the issue of trust.

Whom Not to Trust

The heart of the matter is this: When someone offers you a solution to any financial problem, your first thought should be to wonder "What's in it for him or her?" If you want to solve your problem, there should certainly be individuals available to help you—and whom you approach. This might sound slightly paranoid. However, soon-to-be retirees (and retirees) ought to embrace a little paranoia when it comes to their finances. Scams are rampant among the newly retired, since retirees have a large nest egg and often aren't certain what to do with it.

But even legitimate advisers can give you advice that does more to line their pockets than to help your retirement. If you find yourself fielding financial advice, sales pitches, and a megawatt smile when you did not seek out the adviser, tread cautiously. No one can possibly care about your retirement more than you do, so anyone who offers you an unsolicited solution is probably going to profit from it somehow. That doesn't necessarily mean he's untrustworthy. It just means that you need to be sure you understand what you are getting into.

ASK THE EXPERT

According to Julie Jason, retirement expert and chief investment officer for Jackson, Grant Investment Advisers, Inc., many people looking for financial advice will consider trustworthiness as their first criterion in hiring a financial adviser. However, Julie suggests that all prospective clients should focus on the skills and knowledge that an adviser can offer before worrying about the issue of trust—because trustworthiness can be more easily faked than skills and knowledge.

When it comes to trusting your financial adviser, remember that they will be your ally, not your friend, and that you have the ultimate responsibility to understand what is happening with your money.

Types of Financial Advisers

There are really only four types of advisers:

1. Financial planners
2. Insurance agents
3. Registered investment advisers
4. Registered representatives

However, any adviser can be licensed to handle multiple services or products.

Let's meet each of these types of advisers and learn what kind of advice you can expect from them.

Financial Planners

This is the most loosely defined of all the types of advisers you may encounter. Because there is no regulatory body overseeing self-proclaimed financial planners, anyone can hang up a shingle declaring herself a financial planner.

However, many of these people have gone through the certification necessary to become a Certified Financial Planner (CFP). In order to earn a certification, a financial planner must complete an educational requirement, pass an examination, have at least three years of experience as a financial planner, and agree to the CFP Board's Code of Ethics and Standards of Conduct. The ethics requirement asks for disclosure regarding any previous involvement in unethical practices, and potential CFPs can be barred from certification based on investigation into such actions. Certified Financial Planners are also required to fulfill continuing education requirements to maintain certification.

Okay, you may be saying, but what exactly does a financial planner do? A financial planner, whether a CFP or not, can potentially help clients with anything from saving for college to handling retirement income to estate planning—or do all three (and more) at the same time. By choosing a financial planner as your adviser, you can find someone who has specialized in the particular planning issue you are facing.

THE RISE OF THE MONEY COACH

In the years since this book was first published, the field of "money coaching" has exploded. This newly popular type of financial adviser offers both practical financial management tips and advice as well as psychological coaching to help clients understand and overcome disordered financial behavior. Like career coaching, money coaching is about helping you to better understand your situation so you can make wiser decisions now and in the future. However, money coaches generally do not offer recommendations about investments or portfolio management services, as you can expect from more traditional financial advisers.

Money coaches can help clients to become better money managers. They can also potentially help clients to prepare for retirement, although that is generally not a money coach's primary focus. However, it's important to remember that this field is currently unregulated in any way. There is one certification available for money coaches (the Certified Money Coach, CMC® designation), but it is not required by any governing body. Which means anyone can refer to themselves as a money coach. (Full disclosure: I personally offer money coaching services at EmilyGuyBirken.com.)

The fact that financial planning is loosely defined and unregulated means that you will have to work hard to make sure you completely understand what kinds of products, services, and advice your planner can offer and exactly how payment works. Right now, let's focus on how a financial planner gets paid.

UNDERSTANDING FINANCIAL PLANNER FEES

Fees for financial planning services can vary greatly from planner to planner. In general, there are three different ways that a planner can be paid:

1. **COMMISSION.** This is the most common type of financial planning fee, and it can cause a great deal of confusion among clients shopping for a planner. A commission-based financial planner will be paid when you purchase a particular product through him or her. While there is absolutely nothing wrong with hiring a planner who works on commission, it can be easier for such a planner to conceal potential conflicts of interest. That means a commission-based planner could potentially steer you toward products with higher commissions rather than the products that best fit your needs. If you end up working with a commission-based financial planner, make certain that you understand how your adviser will be paid based on the various products you are offered.

2. **FEE-ONLY.** Fee-only financial planners are often touted as the best alternative for clients, since they are paid directly by clients, rather than based on the products they sell. This means it can be easier to trust that their advice is objective, as their compensation is not based upon selling any particular product. However, there are various ways that clients can pay those fees:

   - **PERCENTAGE OF THE ACCOUNT VALUE**—Planners who are paid this way charge a fee based on a small percentage of your account value, generally between 0.5 percent and 2.5 percent. The benefit to this type of fee is that your planner has a built-in incentive to grow your money and minimize your losses because it affects his bottom line. However, depending on the size of your portfolio, even a small percentage can take an unwelcome bite out of your nest egg.

   - **HOURLY RATE**—An hourly rate is just what it sounds like: You pay your planner an hourly fee for his time, during which he'll advise you on the best way to allocate your assets to meet your particular financial goals. It will then be up to you to follow through on the advice. Hourly rates for financial planners can vary widely, ranging from \$150 per hour to over \$300 per hour.

• **FLAT FEE**—This is similar to an hourly rate, except it can be a better option for those who are more overwhelmed or confused by their options. You will pay your planner a flat fee in order to crunch the numbers for a particular financial issue or goal (like creating your retirement plan) and then provide you with the various alternatives available to you, as well as the pros and cons of each one. If you have never met with a financial planner, finding one who is willing to work on your retirement plan with you for a flat fee can be a great starting point.

FINDING A FEE-ONLY FINANCIAL PLANNER

Many financial experts recommend only working with fee-only financial planners, since you can feel confident that their advice is objective. One good resource for finding a fee-only planner in your area is NAPFA, the National Association of Personal Financial Advisors (www.napfa.org).

3. **FEE-BASED.** This sounds remarkably similar to fee-only. However, fee-based planners are actually compensated both through fees paid directly by their clients and through commissions from the sales or recommendations of specific products. This hybrid approach can be very confusing to clients, so it's important to understand exactly how your fee-based planner receives compensation. (I will talk about what specific questions to ask regarding compensation later on in this chapter.)

Insurance Agents

Insurance agents are licensed within their states to sell life insurance products. These products can include everything from traditional life insurance to retirement income products, such as the annuities we discussed in Chapter 3. Insurance agents (who can also be known as insurance producers) are paid almost exclusively by commission, which means that any advice you receive from one should be taken with a grain of salt.

Licensing for insurance agents varies from state to state, but qualifying for the license includes passing an examination and a background check, and meeting continuing education requirements. This means that insurance agents in each state are regulated by their state insurance commissioners. However, state regulation of insurance, particularly as it applies to consumer protection, has historically had low standards. These consumer protection standards prohibit insurance agents from actively using unfair or deceptive practices, like misrepresenting the terms of a particular product or the financial standing of the company selling that product. But these standards do not require agents to try to find products that best fit their clients' needs.

The National Association of Insurance Commissioners (NAIC) has created a Suitability in Annuity Transactions Model Regulation (MDL-275), which has been adopted by forty-seven states as of 2019. This regulation requires insurance agents to assess your financial status to determine if a particular annuity or other insurance product is suitable for your situation prior to recommending it. (To find out whether your state has adopted the NAIC suitability regulation, visit www.naic.org.)

No matter what the regulations governing your state may be, it's up to you to ensure that you completely understand any product you purchase to determine if it fits your goals and objectives.

Some financial planners are also licensed as insurance agents, which means that you can consult with them regarding general advice, as well as insurance products. Tread carefully, however, because the loosely defined nature of financial planning means that licensed insurance agents can legally call themselves financial planners, without having any other type of financial education, background, or license. This is yet another reason why it is so important to understand how your financial adviser is compensated.

ASK THE EXPERT

Jeff Rose, Certified Financial Planner and personal finance blogger at *Good Financial Cents* (www.goodfinancialcents.com), advises prospective clients to ask exactly how their adviser gets paid. Jeff states, "When you ask point blank about compensation, see what response you get. If they can't clearly articulate how they are paid, that's a major red flag. It's time to move on to someone more upfront."

Registered Investment Advisers

These advisers provide their clients with both investment advice and portfolio management services, which are services you can find among some financial planners. The difference is that registered investment advisers have a fiduciary duty to manage their client's money. That means that not only must a registered investment adviser's advice be suitable for your situation; the adviser is also legally required to put your interests above her own. As a fiduciary, the law requires that your adviser have an ongoing responsibility to your money past the initial recommendation for a product, that your adviser must be able to provide reasonable and independent grounds for any particular investment advice, and that she must disclose any potential conflicts of interest and be completely upfront about her compensation.

In many ways, registered investment advisers are the most regulated financial advisers. Since registered investment advisers must adhere to the fiduciary standard, you can feel confident that the advice you receive is objective and that your money is in ethical hands.

So why isn't everyone consulting a registered investment adviser? It comes down to cost. Registered investment advisers tend to work with extremely wealthy clients with complex financial situations. You'll usually find that the cost of doing business with such an adviser is more expensive than you would like.

That is not to say that it's not worth your time to seek out a registered investment adviser. Take the time to interview one (or several) and find out if their services and fees will fit your needs. The website

Find Your Independent Advisor (www.findyourindependentadvisor.com/ FindAdvisor) offers tips and pointers for finding an adviser, as well as questions to ask to determine if you have found a good fit. (Full disclosure: *Find Your Independent Advisor* is managed by the broker-dealer Charles Schwab & Co.)

Registered Representatives

These advisers are often called stockbrokers or brokers. They are licensed to buy and sell securities, such as stocks, bonds, and mutual funds. Registered representatives generally work for or are affiliated with a broker-dealer, which is a company or firm that trades securities for clients (this is the broker half) and on its own behalf (the dealer half). These advisers (who are often simply referred to as "reps") are licensed through FINRA, the Financial Industry Regulatory Authority. Since reps are regulated by FINRA, it is possible for potential clients to look up a particular adviser's background on FINRA's Central Registration Depository at www.finra.org. (I highly recommend doing such a background check on any financial adviser that you meet. It can give you a better understanding of his or her experience.)

Although registered representatives must pass background checks, and clients can learn the disclosure histories of their reps through the FINRA website, the standards for these advisers are not nearly as stringent as those for a fiduciary-registered investment adviser. Rather than the fiduciary standard, registered representatives are only required to meet the suitability standard. Under this standard, your representative must believe that any particular recommendation he makes is not only suitable for any investor; but that it is also specifically suitable for your particular goals and objectives.

This suitability obligation does not mean that a representative will be free of conflicts of interest, however. Since representatives generally work for broker-dealers, they will sometimes have a financial incentive to sell the products underwritten by their firm, even if those products are not necessarily the right ones for a particular client. The suitability standard does provide clients with recourse in the event that a rep's recommendation was unsuitable. An unhappy client can complain to the brokerage firm employing the rep, as these firms are required to supervise their representatives.

A registered representative may introduce herself as a financial planner, which generally emphasizes that she also provides general financial advice in addition to the ability to trade securities on a client's behalf. In fact, many financial planners have a patchwork of licensures and qualifications. Taking a meeting with a financial adviser may mean that you are talking to someone who is licensed to sell you an insurance product, who can advise you on how to reach your overall financial goals and objectives, and who can trade securities on your behalf.

UNDERSTANDING THE RISE AND FALL OF THE FIDUCIARY RULE

You may recall the battle in the courts over the Department of Labor's fiduciary rule, which was proposed in April of 2016, scheduled for implementation as of 2017, delayed multiple times between 2017 and 2018, and vacated in a two-to-one decision by the Fifth Circuit Court of Appeals on March 15, 2018. The back-and-forth clash over this rule reflects a serious issue in the financial industry, so it's a good idea to understand what happened and what you can expect because of it.

The fiduciary rule, in essence, would have required any financial professional who provides retirement planning advice or who works with retirement plans, to meet fiduciary requirements. That is, all professionals who sell retirement products or give retirement planning advice would have been required to put their clients' financial interests above their own. This would have replaced the long-standing suitability requirement that simply asks non-fiduciary financial professionals to offer investment recommendations that fit the client's defined needs and objectives.

The fiduciary rule was intended to end the potential for conflicts of interest that occur under the suitability standard. Specifically, the fiduciary rule would have required that financial advisers who work on commission to provide a disclosure agreement, known as a Best Interest Contract Exemption (BICE), if there could be a potential conflict of interest with a recommendation. For instance, under this rule, if your adviser recommended a product that offered her a higher commission or a special bonus, she would have to provide you with a BICE agreement so that you would be fully aware of her compensation for the product. There is no such requirement for transparency under the suitability standard.

Ensuring greater transparency in financial advising is indubitably a good thing. However, implementing this rule would have had an enormous ripple effect on the financial industry. Advisers would have seen greatly increased compliance costs, which could have been devastating to smaller and independent broker-dealers who may not have had the resources, technology, and expertise necessary to meet the requirements. This could have fundamentally changed the American financial industry and reduced the number of advisers and firms available to investors. When the United Kingdom implemented a similar rule in 2011, the number of financial advisers in the industry dropped by 22.5 percent over the next eight years.

The death of the fiduciary rule means that investors must continue to do their own due diligence to ensure they receive the best advice and the best products for their needs.

Interview Questions for Prospective Financial Advisers

The following checklist of interview questions can help you find the person who will be your ally in creating a retirement you'll love.

- What is your background and experience?
  You will want to see that your prospective adviser already has several years of experience under her belt and has worked through various market ups and downs.

- Please explain what licenses and certifications you hold.
  This question will help you to understand what type of adviser you are interviewing. It's entirely possible that your adviser has multiple licenses

and certifications, which means that she may be governed by several regulatory agencies.

- How are you compensated?

  If you ask only one question during your interview of potential advisers, make it this one. Understanding precisely how any one adviser will be paid allows you to compare her with others that you interview.

- What is your investment philosophy? What strategies do you use?

  These are good questions to ask even if you are not sure of your own investment philosophy and strategies. Your potential adviser should be able to explain what she considers to be important in investing. If any aspect of the adviser's answer to this question is unclear, ask for clarification.

- Describe your ideal client.

  If you've found the right adviser, you'll hear a description that sounds remarkably like you. If you are not like every other client among your adviser's customers, it's unlikely she'll be able to serve your needs well.

- What is your area of expertise?

  Some advisers focus on investments to help workers start to build their nest egg, others help their clients with estate planning, and still others earn their bread and butter on planning for the transition to retirement. Find an adviser who specializes in your needs.

- Can you show me some sample portfolios?

  If your adviser balks at giving you some samples and instead tries to reassure you that she makes X percent for her clients each year, thank her for her time and lose her business card. Reassurances may sound good, but you want to see the specific dollars and cents of what she has been doing.

- Please tell me what you see as my financial goals and objectives.

  Having your prospective adviser tell you what she has heard regarding the goals and objectives you have already outlined can not only tell you how well she was listening; it can also help you to better understand exactly what it is you want if you have not been able to articulate it yourself.

CHAPTER 4 TAKEAWAYS

☑ There are a number of professions that fall under the loosely defined term of "financial planner." Because of this, it's important you focus on your adviser's expertise, background, skills, and knowledge, rather than on a sense of trustworthiness, since competence is much harder to fake than trustworthiness.

☑ The four main types of financial professional you are likely to meet are:

1. Financial planners
2. Insurance agents
3. Registered investment advisers
4. Registered representatives

☑ Financial planning is loosely regulated, but any adviser carrying the Certified Financial Planner (CFP) designation has met the standards and ongoing requirements set by the CFP Board. Financial planners can help clients with any number of financial management needs, from estate planning to investing for retirement.

☑ Financial planners can be paid via commission, via direct fee (known as fee-only), or with a hybrid of the two, known as fee-based.

☑ Insurance agents are licensed by their state to sell insurance products, such as annuities. Financial planners are sometimes licensed as insurance agents as well, meaning you can receive investment advice and purchase annuity products from the same adviser.

☑ Registered investment advisers (RIAs) provide their clients with both investment advice and portfolio management services, and they are held to a fiduciary standard, meaning they are required to put their clients' financial interests above their own.

☑ Registered representatives are licensed to buy and sell securities on your behalf. They are held to a suitability standard, rather than a fiduciary standard.

☑ The Department of Labor's now-defunct fiduciary rule would have required any financial professional who works with retirement accounts to meet the fiduciary standard. However, the rule was ultimately vacated after several years of back-and-forth court battles, meaning investors are responsible for understanding their adviser's potential conflicts of interest.

☑ It is important to interview potential advisers to make sure you find a good fit. Asking how your potential adviser gets paid is the most important question, but you can also ensure you find the right professional by asking about their background and certification, investment philosophy, and ideal client. You can also request a sample portfolio to help you understand what your adviser does for his or her clients.

What to Do When

YEARS TO RETIREMENT	WHAT TO DO
Five	Set up times to interview several financial advisers and settle on one who will work well with you. Use the interview questions in this chapter.
Four through one	Meet at least once a year with your financial adviser to assess your retirement strategy.

2

The Government Giveth (and Taketh Away)

CHAPTER 5

What to Expect from Social Security

WHAT YOU'LL LEARN IN THIS CHAPTER

Social Security is an important part of your retirement plan, but there are a number of myths and misconceptions about the program that can leave you vulnerable to less-than-ideal claiming strategies. In this chapter, we'll discuss exactly how Social Security works on both the taxpayer and beneficiary side. You will understand why reports of the program's imminent demise tend to be overblown and why you do not need to worry that there will be no benefits available for your retirement. Finally, you will learn how timing, spousal, and survivor benefits, working in retirement, and taxation of benefits can affect the amount you will receive from Social Security.

Social Security is in the news a lot, and that can make you worry. The near-constant political hand-wringing about the sustainability of the program might have you concerned about whether your benefits are guaranteed. The fact that Social Security benefits are the major source of income for most of the elderly (representing at least half of the retirement income for 70 percent of single beneficiaries and 50 percent of married couples) may have you concerned about whether your benefits will be enough. And the fact that this is a government program might have you worried that the road to receiving your benefits will be unbearably complicated. This chapter will help you to determine which of these worries are legitimate and which are not. We will discuss in detail how Social Security works, so that you can incorporate your projected benefits into your retirement plan. By the end of this chapter, you will know what you need to do and when in order to maximize your Social Security benefits.

The Mechanics Behind Social Security

You may know that you pay taxes into Social Security and that those taxes are used to pay benefits. However, many Americans are unaware of exactly where these taxes go and how the benefits are paid.

Regularly employed individuals will see 6.2 percent of their gross earnings taxed for Social Security. In addition, your employer kicks in 6.2 percent, making the total tax contribution 12.4 percent of your gross income. However, there is an income limit on Social Security taxation, which as of 2021 is $142,800. Any income you earn above that limit is not taxed. That means that you will pay no more than $8,853.60 (6.2 percent of $142,800) in Social Security taxes in 2021—although the income limit goes up every year. If you are self-employed, you are considered to be both employer and employee, which means you have to pay the full 12.4 percent of Social Security taxes yourself.

WHO'S FICA? WHY'S HE GETTING ALL MY MONEY?

FICA stands for Federal Insurance Contributions Act, and this is the Social Security payroll tax. However, if you bother to do the math, you will notice that FICA takes more than 6.2 percent of your paycheck. That's because in addition to Social Security, FICA also collects 1.45 percent for Medicare Part A. There is no taxable earnings cap for the Medicare portion of FICA, so even workers earning more than $142,800 will see a full 1.45 percent taken from their paychecks.

A common misconception about Social Security is that the taxes you pay are held for your specific future benefits. However, Social Security retirement benefits are set up as a direct transfer from current workers to current beneficiaries. The money you give up in taxes goes to current Social Security beneficiaries. There is no Social Security account with your name on it that is growing with the taxes that you have personally paid.

Between 1985 and 2009, the taxes coming in to pay for Social Security exceeded the expenses for the program. The surplus that came in during those years (and in every year that income exceeded expenses) was placed in the Social Security Trust Fund, where it earned interest.

In 2010, the yearly expenses for the program exceeded the tax revenue brought in, and that is expected to be the case for the foreseeable future. According to the Social Security Administration, the Social Security Trust Fund began losing value as of 2013, and will become entirely depleted by 2034. As of 2020, the cost of Social Security is projected to exceed its total income (which includes earned interest) for the first time since 1982.

Before you start freaking out, remember that the depletion of the Trust Fund is projected, not guaranteed. Additionally, after 2034, each year's tax revenue is projected to be able to pay for 75 percent of the benefits currently promised through to the year 2093.

Congress could reduce or eliminate the projected Social Security shortfall by raising the income limit on Social Security taxation, by making a slight increase in the payroll tax, and/or with a slight increase in normal retirement age (also known as full retirement age).

As of this writing, President Joe Biden has proposed imposing a 12.4 percent Social Security payroll tax on wages above $400,000 per year. (Under his proposal there will be a "donut hole" for incomes between $142,800 and $400,000, where there is no additional payroll tax imposed.) However, considering how difficult it can be to foster bipartisan agreement on Social Security, we might have to wait a while to see those changes take place.

As it currently stands, of every tax dollar you send to Social Security, 85 cents goes to the Trust Fund for current retirees' benefits, and 15 cents goes to the Trust Fund for current beneficiaries of Social Security disability benefits. According to the Social Security Administration, less than 1 percent of your Social Security taxes is spent on managing the program, making it one of the most efficient agencies in the federal government.

UNDERSTANDING THE TRUST FUND

For many of us, the term "trust fund" evokes the image of a physical vault full of cash to which the government adds the money it takes from each paycheck. This is a tough mental image to shake because it is a little disconcerting to recognize that money is nothing more than an idea we all share, and that neither the US government nor Warren Buffett has an underground vault where you can don a swimsuit and do the backstroke through billions of dollars in cash, à la Scrooge McDuck.

But large amounts of money cannot sit around as cash. Not only is that a security risk (you might remember Goldfinger's plan to rob Fort Knox), but money in a vault additionally loses value to inflation. For that money to avoid losing value (and to have a chance to grow), it must be invested. This is why surplus Social Security money that is not needed for current benefits is invested in the safest of all assets: US government debt in the form of T-Bonds.

How Social Security Works for Beneficiaries

Working and paying taxes toward Social Security earns you "credits" through the program. As of 2021, a taxpayer earns one credit for every $1,470 he or she earns at work, up to a maximum of four credits per year. The credit amount is generally readjusted each year. You will need forty total credits (that is, ten years of work) in order to qualify for retirement benefits.

In addition, nonworking spouses are also eligible for benefits based upon the work history of the breadwinner in the family. This is true even in the case of widowed spouses and divorced spouses, with some important caveats.

HOW MUCH WILL YOU GET?

Your Social Security benefits are based upon two things: your earnings history and your age at enrollment.

While you only need to have ten years of work history in order to qualify for retirement benefits, the calculation of your benefits is based upon the thirty-five highest-earning years in your career. That's great news for a sixty-five-year-old retiree who has been working steadily since she was seventeen years old. With forty-eight years of work history to choose from, Social Security will be able to calculate her benefits based on the thirty-five years she made the most money.

If, however, you have less than thirty-five years of work experience, the Social Security Administration uses zeros to create the average for the calculation, lowering your average earnings and your payout. If you don't have thirty-five years of employment history, it's a good idea to continue working to get those zeros replaced in your Social Security calculation.

As for your age, Social Security changes the benefit amount based on whether you retire before or after your normal retirement age. This is the age at which you receive your full benefit, and this age depends upon the year you were born. For the majority of beneficiaries, normal retirement age is between sixty-six and sixty-seven.

The longer you wait to claim your benefits, the more money you will see in your benefit checks (up until age seventy, when the increase stops). This is why it is generally not advisable for you to take Social Security benefits at age sixty-two, even though you are eligible for them at that time. If you take early benefits, your payments will be permanently reduced. In order to collect your full benefit, you will need to wait until you have reached your normal retirement age.

The closer you are to your normal retirement age when you take benefits, the smaller your benefit reduction will be. In addition, if you delay taking benefits past your normal retirement age, then your monthly payments will increase by 8 percent every year that you delay until you reach age seventy. So until you reach your seventieth birthday, the longer you wait to claim your benefits, the more money you will see in each monthly payment.

To find out what your specific monthly benefit will be, the Social Security Administration uses a complex formula to first index your earnings (that is, to adjust your earnings to account for average wage changes over the years), and then to calculate your benefits.

Fortunately, there are a number of very user-friendly calculators and applications on the Social Security website to help you figure out your potential benefits. You can use the benefits calculators at www.ssa.gov/benefits/calculators/ to enter your specific information and learn what you can expect from your benefits. In addition, signing up for a "my Social Security" account at www.ssa.gov/myaccount/ can provide both workers and retirees with a great deal of specific information about your Social Security earnings record and benefits.

Finally, it's important to remember that your benefits are adjusted each year for inflation. This is called the annual cost-of-living adjustment, or COLA. That means that your benefits should have the same buying power every year that you are retired.

Spousal and Survivor Benefits

As mentioned previously, nonworking spouses are eligible for benefits based upon their spouse's earnings record. In general, the spousal benefit is worth 50 percent of the wage earner's benefit—and the nonworking spouse can collect that at the same time the working spouse is collecting her own retirement benefits. That means a retired married couple can collect up to 150 percent of the working spouse's benefit at any time.

But spousal benefits are not only for families where only one spouse worked. It is also possible for a lower-earning spouse to benefit from the higher wages of his partner, if the lower earner's benefit is less than half as much as his higher-earning spouse's benefit. If your spouse earned significantly more than you did during your career, then you are potentially eligible for spousal benefits in addition to your retirement benefits. This spousal benefit is known as the excess spousal benefit, which I will refer to as ESB.

The formula for calculating the ESB is based upon both spouses' primary insurance amount, or PIA. (PIA is defined as the amount of money a beneficiary is eligible to receive upon reaching normal retirement age.) Your ESB is equal to 50 percent of your spouse's PIA, minus your PIA.

> **50% OF SPOUSE'S PIA – YOUR PIA = YOUR ESB**

EXAMPLE:
Leia's PIA is $2,400 and her husband Han's PIA is $1,000.
50% of Leia's PIA – Han's PIA = Han's ESB
(50% of $2,400) – $1,000 = $200

Divorce and Spousal Benefits

Believe it or not, you do not have to still be married to your spouse in order to benefit from his or her Social Security retirement benefits. The Social Security Administration recognizes your right to spousal benefits even if your marriage did not survive. In order for divorcé(e)s to qualify for these benefits, four requirements must be met:

1. Your marriage must have lasted at least ten years.

2. The ex-spouse who is claiming spousal benefits must not have remarried. If you have not remarried but your ex has, you are still eligible for spousal benefits, and the spousal benefits you collect will not affect the benefits that your ex and their new spouse are entitled to.

3. You may collect spousal benefits if your ex-spouse qualifies for their own retirement benefits *even if* your ex has not yet applied for benefits, provided you have been divorced for at least two years prior to the date of your filing for spousal benefits.

4. You must be at least sixty-two.

Survivor Benefits

If you become a widow or widower, you are eligible for survivor benefits through Social Security. No matter what age your spouse was at the time of his or her death, you can apply for these survivor benefits when you reach age sixty (or fifty, if you are disabled).

The amount you are entitled to through a survivor benefit depends on your age at the time of your application for the benefits, as well as the specifics of whether and when the deceased spouse took retirement benefits. If you have reached normal retirement age, then your survivor benefit can potentially be equal to the full amount of your spouse's retirement benefit. However, if you take survivor benefits prior to normal retirement age, then your benefits are reduced. The younger you are when you take survivor benefits, the smaller your monthly benefit checks will be.

Survivor benefits are for any spouse who was married for at least nine months before the covered spouse died, although divorced spouses are eligible for survivor benefits as long as they were married for ten years and the surviving ex-spouse is not remarried. However, if you were married at the time of the death and you were a co-parent with the deceased spouse, or if the death was accidental (either on or off the job), or if the death was during active military duty, then the nine-month length of marriage minimum is waived.

How Working in Retirement Affects Your Benefits

Whether you decide to take a job in retirement just to get out of the house or because you really need to continue bringing in a paycheck, if you have already applied for Social Security benefits, your working income can negatively affect your benefits.

In particular, if you are still working and you start drawing benefits before you reach your normal retirement age, then you will see $1 deducted from your benefits for every $2 you earn over $18,960 (as of 2021). What is possibly a bigger issue is that Social Security does not prorate these deductions. Beneficiaries who make over the income limit will find their benefits completely withheld until they have reached the full benefit reduction amount.

If, however, you wait to begin drawing benefits during the same year that you reach normal retirement age, the income limit is higher ($50,520 for 2021) and the amount your benefits are reduced is lower— $1 for every $3 you earn above that amount. The very month that you reach your normal retirement age, you will be allowed to keep every penny of your benefits, no matter how much money you are earning through other work.

However, even if your benefits are reduced in such a way, the benefit money is not gone forever. Social Security will increase your benefits once you reach your normal retirement age in order to take into account the months you had your benefits withheld.

The effect of working income on your early Social Security benefits is yet another reason why it's truly in your best interest to hold off on applying for benefits until you have reached your normal retirement age.

Taxes and Your Social Security Benefits

We will cover this issue in much greater depth in Chapter 6, but it's important to point out that your Social Security benefits may be subject to taxation. About 40 percent of current retirement beneficiaries pay taxes on their benefits, which can be an important issue to consider while planning your retirement budget. You will only owe taxes on your benefits if your provisional income is over a base amount: $25,000 for single filers, and $32,000 for married couples filing jointly. It's also important to remember that these base amounts have not increased since 1984 and are not tied to inflation, which means more beneficiaries pay taxes on their benefits over time as retirement incomes naturally increase with inflation.

In addition, even though the set base amount is simple to understand, there is a complicated method for determining your provisional income to compare to that base amount. To calculate your provisional income, you will add together your taxable income (which includes distributions from tax-deferred and taxable retirement accounts but does not include distributions from Roth accounts), your tax-exempt interest (such as interest on municipal bonds), and half of your Social Security benefits. If the calculated number is greater than the base amount, then you will owe taxes on a portion no greater than 50 to 85 percent of your Social Security retirement benefits. (Please turn to Chapter 6 for a thorough explanation of the Social Security taxation formula plus worksheets that will help you determine how much you might owe.)

Applying for Benefits

The application for retirement benefits is available online at www.socialsecurity.gov, and the application process is fairly straightforward. Social Security recommends applying for your benefits about three months prior to the date you would like to start receiving your monthly benefit checks. The following is needed:

- Your Social Security number
- Your original birth certificate or other proof of birth
- Proof of US citizenship or lawful alien status if you were not born in the United States
- Your military discharge papers if you served
- A copy of either your W-2 forms or your self-employment tax return of the previous year

In addition to this, you should know that the term "Social Security benefit check" is now a misnomer. As of May 2011, new Social Security recipients have been required to accept their benefits electronically. When you sign up for your benefits, you will need to either provide the Social Security Administration with your bank account information and routing number, or opt for your benefits to be loaded onto a prepaid debit card.

CHAPTER 5 TAKEAWAYS

☑ Social Security retirement benefits are set up as a direct transfer from current workers to current beneficiaries. Workers pay 6.2 percent of their gross earnings in Social Security taxes, up to an income limit of $142,800.

☑ The Social Security Administration projects that the Trust Fund will be depleted by 2034. After that point, the program will only be able to pay 75 percent of currently promised benefits.

☑ The shortfall can be potentially reduced or eliminated by raising the income limit on Social Security taxes, by making a slight payroll tax increase, or by raising the normal retirement age for future beneficiaries.

☑ The size of your benefit is based upon your work history and when you file for benefits. Use the benefits calculators at www.ssa.gov/benefits/calculators/ to learn how much you can expect from your benefits.

☑ If you earned significantly less than your spouse (or ex-spouse in some cases), you may be eligible for spousal benefits.

☑ If you become a widow or widower, you are likely eligible for survivor benefits through Social Security.

☑ Working while collecting Social Security before you have reached your normal retirement age could potentially reduce your benefit amount.

☑ Your Social Security benefits may be subject to taxation, if your provisional income is above $25,000 (for singles) or $32,000 (for married couples).

☑ Apply for retirement benefits online at www.socialsecurity.gov about three months prior to when you would like to begin receiving them.

What to Do When

YEARS TO RETIREMENT	WHAT TO DO
Five	Sign up for a "my Social Security" account at www.ssa.gov/myaccount/ to easily access all of your Social Security records and information.
Five	By the end of the year, calculate your projected Social Security benefits, using the calculators at www.ssa.gov/benefits/calculators/.
One	Three months before you would like to start receiving Social Security benefits, apply for them online at www.socialsecurity.gov. You will need your Social Security number, your original birth certificate, proof of US citizenship, your military discharge papers if you served, and a copy of your W-2 forms or your self-employment tax return for the previous year.

CHAPTER 6

Taxes and Your Retirement Income

WHAT YOU'LL LEARN IN THIS CHAPTER

There is no avoiding the taxman, not even in retirement. Unfortunately, handling your tax burden in retirement can be a very complex endeavor. This chapter will outline for you the various tax issues you may encounter in retirement, including taxation on Social Security benefits, pensions, retirement accounts, annuities, and taxable investments. By the end of this chapter, you will know what to expect from taxes on your retirement income.

While it is possible that your financial adviser can also help you with tax issues (particularly on the investment side of the tax equation), many retirees will find that they need a CPA to help them handle the minutiae of tax preparation in retirement. If you have never worked with a CPA, it's a good idea to start with a referral from either your financial adviser or from friends or colleagues on a similar retirement time frame. Your accountant will know intimate details about your financial life, so you want to be sure you pick one you can trust. As with interviewing a financial adviser (see Chapter 4), you should ask about your prospective accountant's background, education, experience, and how they have helped other retirees in similar situations.

The tax code has very specific rules about how you will pay Uncle Sam depending on the source of your retirement income. We'll discuss each potential source of retirement income and what kind of bite you can expect taxes to take from each one.

Social Security Income

You might expect Social Security to be a tax-free source of retirement income, but as with pretty much any money that passes through your hands, the government wants its share. Unless your retirement income is less than a certain amount, you can expect to pay taxes on anywhere from 50 to 85 percent of a portion of your Social Security benefits.

In order to figure out if you owe Uncle Sam any money, you will calculate your provisional income. This is determined by adding together:

1. One-half of your Social Security benefits, plus
2. All of your other income, including tax-exempt interest. (While tax-exempt interest is included in this calculation, tax-free distributions from your Roth IRA are not.) The amount that you come up with is then compared to the following base amounts in order to determine how much of your Social Security benefits are taxed (if any):

TABLE 6-1:
Base Amounts to Determine Taxable Social Security

IF YOU FILE AS	SINGLE	MARRIED, FILING JOINTLY
Then Your Base Amount Is	$25,000	$32,000
And You Will Owe Taxes on This Percentage of Your Social Security Benefits	50%	50%
Your Additional Amount Is	$34,000	$44,000
And You Will Owe Taxes on This Percentage of Your Social Security Benefits	85%	85%

If your provisional income falls below the lower base amount, then you will owe no taxes on your Social Security benefits. If your provisional income falls between the lower and upper base amounts, you will owe taxes on up to 50 percent of your benefits. And if your provisional income is greater than the upper base amount, then you will owe taxes on no more than 85 percent of your benefits.

WHY YOU SHOULD HIRE AN ACCOUNTANT

No matter how tax-savvy you are or how long you have handled your own returns, it's a good idea to hire a Certified Public Accountant (CPA) to help you navigate the tax code as you near retirement and to help you minimize your tax burden in retirement. Not only will your CPA be able to stay on top of the constantly evolving tax code in a way that no layperson can expect to; she will also know of tax strategies that might never occur to you.

DETERMINING YOUR TAXABLE BENEFITS

Now that you know how to calculate what portion of your Social Security benefits will be taxed, take the time to determine what that portion will be with Worksheet 6–1, adapted from Worksheet 1 of the IRS Publication 915, which you can find at www.irs.gov/pub/irs-pdf/p915.pdf.

Use the projected Social Security benefits you calculated in Chapter 5, as well as the projected retirement income you have discussed with your financial adviser in order to fill out this worksheet.

WORKSHEET 6–1:
IRS Worksheet 1—Figuring Out Your Taxable Benefits

1	Enter your total Social Security benefits	$
2	Enter one-half of line 1	$
3	Enter your other taxable income	$
4	Add lines 2 and 3	$
5	Enter the base amount for your filing status ($25,000 for single filers, $32,000 for married taxpayers filing jointly)	$
6	Subtract line 5 from line 4 (if zero or less, enter 0)	$

7	Enter $9,000 if single or $12,000 if married filing jointly (this number is the difference between the base amount and the additional amount; that is, it's the difference between $25,000 and $34,000 for single filers and the difference between $32,000 and $44,000 for taxpayers who are married, filing jointly)	$
8	Subtract line 7 from line 6 (if zero or less, enter 0)	$
9	Enter the smaller of line 6 or line 7	$
10	Enter one-half of line 9	$
11	Enter the smaller of line 2 or line 10	$
12	Multiply line 8 by 85% (0.85); if line 8 is zero, enter 0	$
13	Add lines 11 and 12	$
14	Multiply line 1 by 85% (0.85)	$
15	Taxable Benefits: Enter the smaller of line 13 or line 14	$

Once you have calculated your taxable benefits, you are still not quite done. The amount you calculate in Worksheet 6–1 (or with Worksheet 1 in IRS Publication 915) simply tells you how much of your Social Security income will be taxable. The taxable amount of your benefits just gives you the number of dollars you will owe taxes on—not how much is taken from your benefits to pay those taxes. Those benefits are taxed at your marginal tax rate.

OKAY, SO HOW MUCH DO YOU OWE?

If your Social Security benefits are taxable, they will be taxed at your marginal tax rate, which is determined based upon your level of income. Marginal tax rates are adjusted each year, and they occasionally go through a major change, as we saw with the passing of the 2017 Tax Cuts and Jobs Act, which lowered the marginal tax rate of five of the seven tax brackets. Use the following chart to determine your marginal tax rate as of 2021:

TABLE 6-2:
2021 Marginal Tax Rates

MARGINAL TAX RATE	SINGLE FILER INCOME	MARRIED, FILING JOINTLY INCOME
10%	up to $9,950	up to $19,900
12%	$9,951 to $40,525	$19,901 to $81,050
22%	$40,526 to $86,375	$81,051 to $172,750
24%	$86,376 to $164,925	$172,751 to $329,850
32%	$164,926 to $209,425	$329,851 to $418,850
35%	$209,426 to $523,600	$418,851 to $628,300
37%	$523,601+	$628,301+

Remember, the marginal tax rate is only the rate you pay on the highest portion of your income. Which is to say, if you fall in the 22 percent tax bracket, you are not taxed 22 percent on all of your income. You are taxed 22 percent on any income above $40,525 (if you are single), you are taxed 12 percent on any income between $9,950 and $40,525, and you are taxed 10 percent on any income below $9,950.

DEFINING YOUR TAX RATE

Throughout this chapter, you will see references to various tax rates. The marginal tax rate refers to the rate you pay on the highest portion of your income. You determine your marginal tax rate by knowing what your tax bracket is. If you and your spouse earn $95,000 per year, you are currently in the 22 percent tax bracket, which means you pay 22 percent tax on every dollar you earn above $81,050—the upper limit for the 12 percent tax bracket. You will only pay 12 percent tax on the income you make between $19,900 and $81,050 (the income floor and ceiling for the 12 percent tax bracket), and 10 percent tax on the income below $19,900 (the maximum income for the 10 percent tax bracket). Your overall tax rate is often referred to as your ordinary income tax rate, which encompasses all that you pay based upon your income tax bracket.

Let's take a look at an example:

Dana and Peter receive Social Security retirement benefits equaling $30,000 per year for the couple. In addition to their Social Security benefits, they also have additional taxable income of $32,000 per year. Here's how Dana and Peter would calculate their provisional income:

1/2 of Dana and Peter's Social Security Benefits:	$15,000
+ Their additional taxable income:	$32,000
= Their provisional income:	$47,000

Their total taxable amount is clearly above the $44,000 upper base amount limit. Let's use IRS Worksheet 1 again to determine how much of their benefits are taxable:

WORKSHEET 6-2:

IRS Worksheet 1—Figuring Dana and Peter's Taxable Benefits

1	Enter their total Social Security benefits	$30,000
2	Enter one-half of line 1	$15,000
3	Enter their other taxable income	$32,000
4	Add lines 2 and 3	$47,000
5	Enter the base amount for your filing status ($25,000 for single filers, $32,000 for married taxpayers filing jointly)	$32,000
6	Subtract line 5 from line 4 (if zero or less, enter 0)	$15,000
7	Enter $9,000 if single or $12,000 if married filing jointly (this number is the difference between the base amount and the additional amount; that is, it's the difference between $25,000 and $34,000 for single filers and the difference between $32,000 and $44,000 for taxpayers who are married, filing jointly)	$12,000
8	Subtract line 7 from line 6 (if zero or less, enter 0)	$3,000
9	Enter the smaller of line 6 or line 7	$12,000
10	Enter one-half of line 9	$6,000
11	Enter the smaller of line 2 or line 10	$6,000
12	Multiply line 8 by 85% (0.85) (if line 8 is zero, enter 0)	$2,550
13	Add lines 11 and 12	$8,550
14	Multiply line 1 by 85% (0.85)	$25,500
15	Taxable Benefits: Enter the smaller of line 13 or line 14	$8,550

In this case, Dana and Peter will owe taxes on $8,550 of their Social Security retirement benefits. Their provisional income of $47,000 puts the couple in the 12 percent tax bracket. That means the $8,550 of taxable Social Security benefits will be taxed at 12 percent, meaning they will owe $1,026 in taxes on their Social Security benefits ($8,550 × 12% = $1,026).

This means that of their $30,000 in Social Security benefits, Dana and Peter will get to keep $28,974 ($30,000 − $1,026 = $28,974).

Income from an Employer Pension Plan

If you are fortunate enough to be covered under an employer's pension plan, then your payments from that pension may be either fully or partially taxable. Your pension is fully taxable if it was funded with pre-tax income, which is the case for the majority of pensioners. That means your pension payments will be taxed at your ordinary income tax rate. On the other hand, if any part of your pension was funded with after-tax dollars, then your pension will only be partially taxable in retirement. In order to determine exactly what portion of your pension is taxable, you will need to fill out the (poorly named) IRS Simplified Method Worksheet, currently found on page 28 of the 1040 Instruction Manual (www.irs.gov/pub/irs-pdf/i1040gi.pdf).

401(k) and Traditional IRA Distributions

Because you funded your 401(k) and traditional IRA with pre-tax money, every withdrawal you make is taxed at your ordinary income tax rate. However, if you withdraw money from either a 401(k) or a traditional IRA before you have reached the magical (and somewhat arbitrary) age of fifty-nine-and-a-half, then you will owe a 10 percent early-withdrawal penalty on the amount you withdraw, as well as your ordinary income tax.

You are not required to take any distributions (withdrawals) from these tax-deferred accounts just because you reach age fifty-nine-and-a-half. That is simply the earliest age that you may withdraw money penalty-free.

As we discussed in detail in Chapter 3, you are required to take a minimum amount from your tax-deferred retirement accounts once you reach age seventy-two. The required minimum distributions will change each year depending on the remaining balance in your account and your age.

Because any distribution you take from your tax-deferred accounts is taxable as ordinary income and can therefore negatively affect your tax burden in retirement, we'll talk later in this chapter about the best way to handle your retirement in order to be as tax-efficient as possible.

WHY FIFTY-NINE-AND-A-HALF?

The beginning withdrawal age of fifty-nine-and-a-half is a somewhat arbitrary choice. Congress used this number because life insurance actuarial tables consider you to be sixty years old once you have reached fifty-nine and six months, and at the time the rules were put in place, sixty was a relatively common age for retirement.

Roth IRAs and Roth 401(k)s

One of the big benefits to investing in a Roth IRA or Roth 401(k) is that the tax burden is front-loaded. You invest after-tax dollars in your Roth account, which means that distributions taken after you have reached age fifty-nine-and-a-half are entirely tax-free. In addition, there is no required minimum distribution for Roth accounts, so you can take these distributions whenever you like—provided you have reached the age of fifty-nine-and-a-half and you have held the account for at least five years. Early withdrawals, however, are subject to a 10 percent federal tax penalty, just like with traditional IRAs and 401(k)s.

Taxable Investments: Stocks, Bonds, and Mutual Funds

If, in addition to your tax-deferred or tax-free retirement accounts, you have also put money in taxable investments, then that can also affect your taxable retirement income. These investments are taxed annually, whether you're retired or not. Here's a breakdown of how non-tax-sheltered stocks, bonds, and mutual funds are each taxed.

STOCKS

A stock represents ownership in a company. When you own stock in a company, you make money when the company does, and the goal of owning a stock is to buy it at a low price and sell it at a high price. Stocks that you own outside of tax-sheltered investments like 401(k)s and IRAs are taxed in two ways: when or if you receive dividends (a regularly paid distribution of the company's earnings to stockholders) and when you make a profit on the sale of your stock. This second type of profit is known as a capital gain.

Capital gains are taxed differently depending upon whether you have held the stock for less than one year, which is considered a short-term capital gain, or more than one year, which is considered a long-term capital gain. The 2017 Tax Cuts and Jobs Act changed how both short-term and long-term capital gains are taxed. Short-term gains and ordinary dividends are taxed at your ordinary income tax rate. Qualified dividends and all long-term capital gains are taxed at the long-term capital gains rate. Like ordinary income, long-term capital gains tax rates are based upon your income level. However, there are currently only three tax brackets for long-term capital gains tax:

TABLE 6-3:
2021 Long-Term Capital Gains Tax Brackets

TAX RATE	SINGLE FILER INCOME	MARRIED, FILING JOINTLY INCOME
0%	up to $40,400	up to $80,800
15%	$40,401 to $445,850	$80,801 to $501,600
20%	$445,851+	$501,601+

If you earn less than $40,400 as a single filer or $80,800 as a married couple filing jointly, then you will owe no taxes on long-term capital gains.

BONDS

A bond represents a company's debt. An investor buying a bond has in effect loaned the company money, and in exchange, the investor will receive regular interest payments, as well as repayment of the principal when the bond matures.

While there are some types of bonds that are exempt from taxation—specifically, municipal bonds can be entirely tax-free—the majority of bond investors will be taxed at their ordinary income tax rate when they receive their interest payments.

MUTUAL FUNDS

Put simply, a mutual fund is a pool of stocks and bonds, which means that taxation on mutual funds reflects the various types of investments within the fund. You may receive dividends from your mutual fund, which will generally be taxed at the rates listed previously. You will also receive capital gains distributions. No matter how long you have owned shares in the mutual fund, your capital gains through a mutual fund will be taxed at the long-term capital gains rate.

Annuities

If you have decided to invest in an annuity for your retirement, the tax implications can be somewhat complicated. Let's look at how you will pay taxes on both immediate and deferred annuities.

TAXATION ON IMMEDIATE ANNUITIES

When you purchase an immediate annuity, a portion of every check you receive is from the principal you paid, and a portion is from the interest your investment has earned. Uncle Sam does not tax the return of your principal, assuming that you purchased your annuity with after-tax dollars, since that would mean you'd be paying taxes twice on the same money. However, the IRS views the portion of your payments that come from interest to be ordinary income, and therefore you are taxed at your ordinary income tax rate on those portions of the payment.

But how do the IRS and the insurance company holding your annuity determine how much of each payment is principal and how much is interest? Using your life expectancy (as determined by the IRS) and the payout time frame, the insurance company will determine what your exclusion ratio will be. The exclusion ratio is the percentage of your annuity payments that can be excluded from your taxes, since that percentage is considered to be the portion of your payment coming from your principal. In order to calculate the exclusion ratio, the insurance company will divide your investment amount by the total payments you are expected to receive over the payout time frame.

TABLE 6-4:
Determining Tax on Immediate Annuity Income

Investment Amount	$100,000
Payout Period	Lifetime
Life Expectancy According to the IRS	18 years (at age 65)
Annual Payment	$7,800 ($650 per month)
Total Payments over Life Expectancy (18 Years)	$140,400
Exclusion Ratio (Investment/Total Payments)	$100,000/$140,400 = 0.712 or 71.2%

Deferred Annuities

The big difference between immediate and deferred annuities is when you begin to receive payments. Deferred annuities hold onto your initial investment for a period of time known as the surrender period, during which time your investment should be earning interest. That interest grows tax-deferred until you begin to take payments from your annuity. There are three ways that you can receive your payments from a deferred annuity, and each one has its own tax implications:

1. **AT-WILL WITHDRAWALS.** Once you have reached the end of your surrender period (the time during which you may not withdraw money from a deferred annuity), you may take withdrawals in any amount you like, whenever you like. These withdrawals are considered to come from the earnings on your principal, and are taxed at your ordinary income tax rate.

2. **A LUMP-SUM WITHDRAWAL.** If you decide to access all of the money in your deferred annuity at once, anything that you have earned in interest is considered ordinary income and is taxed at your ordinary tax rate. For instance, if you invested $100,000 in a deferred annuity, and it has grown to $250,000 by the time you are ready to withdraw it in a lump sum, then you will owe taxes on $150,000. This also means that the $150,000 will be added to your earned income for the year, pushing you into a higher tax bracket.

3. **AN IMMEDIATE ANNUITY.** After the end of the surrender period, you have the option of converting your deferred annuity into an immediate annuity, which means you will receive regular payments. As with a typical immediate annuity, you will be taxed on your payments based upon the exclusion ratio outlined previously.

How to Mitigate Your Tax Burden

Now that you know all the ways Uncle Sam will take a bite out of your retirement income, it's time to talk about ways to reduce that tax burden. There are things you can do now and after you retire to ensure you keep as much of your retirement income as possible.

Just as it is important to diversify your investments, it's also crucial to diversify your tax burden. That way, you can space out when you pay taxes rather than deal with them all at once. There are two important strategies to consider when diversifying your tax burden: strategic use of a Roth IRA or Roth 401(k) and tax-efficient asset allocation among your investments. We'll discuss each of these in turn.

INVEST IN A ROTH IRA

Roth IRAs are excellent vehicles for retirement savings. Like their traditional counterparts, Roth IRAs offer tax advantages and tax-free growth. However, instead of funding these accounts with pre-tax money and paying taxes at the time of withdrawal, you fund Roth accounts with post-tax dollars, and you owe nothing to Uncle Sam when the money is withdrawn (provided you meet the withdrawal requirements). In addition, Roth IRAs do not have any required minimum distributions, which means you can allow your money to continue to grow tax-free for as long as you like. That also means you can pass on the assets within your Roth IRA to heirs, who will also be able to make tax-free withdrawals, although inherited Roth IRAs are subject to required minimum distributions. Finally, distributions from your Roth IRA are not included in your taxable income, which means retirement income you pull from your Roth IRA will not affect your Social Security benefits in any way.

All in all, it's an excellent idea to have at least a portion of your nest egg invested in a Roth account. In fact, many advisers suggest that pre-retirees should invest in both Roth and traditional accounts, as that will allow them greater flexibility in retirement.

If you do not already have a Roth IRA, you can set one up with your financial adviser and spend the next few years before you retire making contributions to the new account. The only downside to this is that the yearly contribution limit (see Table 6–5) encompasses all IRAs you may own, meaning you must divide that contribution amount among all IRAs you own, whether they are traditional or Roth. In addition, there are income limits on Roth IRA contributions (also listed in Table 6–5), so some high earners are not able to make contributions to Roth accounts.

TABLE 6-5:

2021 Roth IRA Contribution Limits

FILING STATUS	INCOME LIMIT	CONTRIBUTION LIMIT
Married Filing Jointly	Less than $198,000	$6,000 ($7,000 if over 50)
Married Filing Jointly	$198,001 to $208,000	a reduced amount*
Married Filing Jointly	More than $208,000	0
Single	Less than $125,000	$6,000 ($7,000 if over 50)
Single	$125,001 to $140,000	a reduced amount*
Single	More than $140,000	0

* In order to determine the reduced amount that you may contribute, visit www.irs.gov/publications/p590a for the IRS formula to determine the reduction.

If opening a new Roth IRA will not allow you to put as much away as you'd like, you also have the option of converting a traditional IRA into a Roth. However, you will owe ordinary income tax on the amount of money that you convert.

It is possible to pay the taxes owed from your IRA so that you do not have to pay those taxes out of pocket. However, it is generally a better idea to leave your IRA funds where they are so they can continue to grow for you. In addition, the money you convert will be added to your adjusted gross income for the year, potentially pushing you into a higher tax bracket without any real increase in your income to help you pay for the rise in your taxes.

Deciding whether to convert one of your traditional IRAs into a Roth is something you should discuss with both your financial adviser and your accountant. However, for a quick and dirty calculation on the benefits of this type of conversion, check out Bankrate's Convert IRA to Roth Calculator at www.bankrate.com/retirement/calculators/convert-ira-roth-calculator.

TAX-EFFICIENT ASSET ALLOCATION

You can further allocate your stocks, bonds, and mutual funds within your tax-sheltered (e.g., IRAs and 401(k)s) and taxable accounts.

As we discussed previously, bonds tend to have the highest tax burden, because you are taxed at your ordinary income rate on interest payments from bonds. On the other hand, most of the income from stocks will be taxed at the lower, long-term capital gains rate. Clients who have both tax-sheltered and taxable retirement accounts should divvy up their assets in the most tax-efficient way possible. That would mean placing high-yield bonds—which could raise your taxes—into your IRA and placing your stocks and tax-exempt municipal bonds into taxable accounts, since they will keep your tax burden low.

The exact alchemy for creating the most tax-efficient portfolio possible is not easy to figure out—and it will be different from one retiree to another. That's why it's important to discuss this subject with your financial adviser.

CHAPTER 6 TAKEAWAYS

☑ Hiring an accountant to help you navigate taxes in retirement can potentially minimize your tax burden and reduce your IRS-related stress.

☑ A portion of your Social Security benefits may be taxable, depending on your total income. If you owe taxes on a portion of your Social Security benefits, you will pay your marginal tax rate on the taxable portion.

☑ Most pensioners will find that all of their pension income is fully taxable, but some will pay taxes on only a portion of their pension. The IRS Simplified Method Worksheet contained in the 1040 Instruction Manual can help you determine your pension's tax burden.

☑ Distributions taken from your tax-deferred accounts (such as your 401(k) or traditional IRA) are taxable as ordinary income, provided you have waited to take distributions until after reaching age fifty-nine-and-a-half. Distributions prior to that milestone are subject to a 10 percent early-withdrawal penalty.

☑ Roth IRA and Roth 401(k) account distributions are entirely tax-free, provided you have waited to take distributions until after reaching age fifty-nine-and-a-half.

☑ Capital gains refers to the profit you make from the sale of a stock. Short-term capital gains (when you have owned the stock for less than one year) are taxed at your ordinary income rate. Long-term capital gains are taxed based upon your income, as well, but there are only three income brackets, and investors with an income lower than $40,400 for single filers or $80,800 for married couples pay 0 percent tax on their long-term capital gains.

☑ How you are taxed on your annuity depends in part on whether it is an immediate or deferred annuity. With immediate annuities, you are only taxed on the growth, and the amount you paid in principal is excluded from taxation. For deferred annuities, the type of withdrawal you make will determine how your withdrawal is taxed.

☑ Some strategies for mitigating your tax burden in retirement include investing in a Roth IRA (to ensure tax-free distributions in retirement) and using a tax-efficient asset allocation strategy in your tax-deferred and taxable investments.

What to Do When

YOUR AGE	WHAT TO DO
Fifty-nine-and-a-half	You may begin to make penalty-free withdrawals from your tax-advantaged accounts (including Roth and traditional IRAs and 401(k)s) if you have held them for at least five years.

CHAPTER 7

What to Expect from Medicare

WHAT YOU'LL LEARN IN THIS CHAPTER

Navigating the specifics of enrolling in Medicare, determining what kind of care is covered, and understanding Medicare payment limits can be tricky. However, although Medicare is governed by a dizzying number of rules, no one issue is particularly difficult to understand. By the end of this chapter, you will not only be able to explain the differences between Medicare Parts A, B, C, and D; you will also understand what to expect from Medicare during your retirement, and you will have a better idea of how much money you will need to budget for healthcare in retirement.

Understanding Original Medicare

For people nearing retirement, Medicare is often a confusing and stressful subject. A 2018 survey by Nationwide Retirement Institute found that 72 percent of older Americans wish they understood Medicare better, which indicates that they don't fully understand the coverage options that they plan to sign up for. Add in the inherent complexity involved with any kind of bureaucracy that services over 59 million beneficiaries, and it's no wonder so many potential beneficiaries are confused.

You may already know that Medicare is a health insurance program for Americans who are age sixty-five or older and that it was signed into law in 1965. You may also realize that anyone who has been on Social

Security disability for at least two years is eligible for Medicare. You may even have heard something about Medicare Parts A through D.

However, understanding your rights through Medicare can be a little overwhelming. Medicare is an imperfect and stitched-together program that requires some work and diligence on the part of the beneficiary to ensure proper coverage and care. It is for this reason that soon-to-be retirees—even those who are years away from blowing out sixty-five candles on their birthday cakes—should familiarize themselves with their Medicare options. That will help with both financial and healthcare planning (more on the latter in Chapter 8) and help make the decision-making process much simpler when enrolling in Medicare.

THE FUTURE OF AMERICAN HEALTHCARE

At the time of this writing (November 2020), healthcare has become something of a political football, and it is impossible to know exactly what to expect from our healthcare options while the politicians continue to argue. Though we cannot predict what the future healthcare options for Americans under the age of sixty-five will look like, the mechanics of traditional Medicare will most likely maintain their current shape and stability over the coming years, even if specific details change.

Medicare Part A

The Original Medicare program consists of Parts A and B. Part A is also known as hospital insurance; it (partially) covers inpatient hospital care, inpatient care in a skilled nursing facility, home healthcare, and hospice care. If you need to stay in a hospital, if you need skilled nursing care (after certain other obligations have been met) either in a facility or at home, or if you need hospice care, then Medicare Part A will cover some portion of your care.

COST OF MEDICARE PART A

The good news is that the majority of Americans don't owe a premium for Part A. If you or your spouse worked for at least ten years in a position that paid taxes to Medicare, then you have already paid for Medicare Part A and will have to spend no money out of pocket on Part A premiums. Even if you are not eligible for premium-free Medicare Part A, you can still enroll and pay for your premiums out of pocket. These monthly premiums cost $471 as of 2021. However, in order to enroll in Medicare Part A if you have not paid into it through your taxes, you must also enroll in Part B, which costs most people $148.50 per month as of 2021.

The long and short of it is that you may be looking at a monthly payment of up to $619.50 (as of 2021) for your Medicare benefits if you are not eligible for premium-free Part A.

ADDITIONAL PART A PREMIUM RULES

Medicare rules state that anyone who has paid into Medicare taxes for at least ten years does not have to pay premiums for Part A upon reaching age sixty-five. That is because a beneficiary needs to have forty quarters of coverage (QCs), which means that he or she paid into Medicare taxes for forty total quarters—which equals ten years. But what if you paid Medicare taxes for any amount under ten years? For those individuals with between thirty and thirty-nine QCs (7.5 to 9.75 years of Medicare-tax-paying employment), the monthly premium cost for Part A is only $259 per month as of 2021. Anyone with fewer than thirty QCs must pay the full monthly premium amount.

WHAT DOES MEDICARE PART A COVER?

So let's say that you are eligible for Medicare Part A. What exactly does that coverage get you?

As I mentioned previously, Part A covers hospital, skilled nursing facility, home health, and hospice care. However, each of these types of care comes with rules, restrictions, and deductibles. Here's a basic breakdown of what Medicare pays for each type of care.

THE BENEFIT PERIOD

The amount that Medicare will pay depends on the number of days you need inpatient care during what's known as the benefit period. The benefit period refers to the time that you are in a hospital or skilled nursing facility (i.e., a nursing home) due to a particular illness or injury. Your benefit period begins on the day you are admitted into the hospital or facility as an inpatient and lasts until you have been out of the hospital for sixty consecutive days.

This means that if you go home after heart trouble puts you in the hospital and then return to the hospital for more tinkering with your ticker within two months of checking out, you are still within the original benefit period—which will affect what and how much Medicare will cover. For this reason, having two benefit periods for the same illness will be cheaper for you out of pocket.

HOSPITAL CARE

1. **THE DEDUCTIBLE:** For each benefit period you use, you must pay a deductible before Medicare coverage kicks in. The deductible amount (as well as every other amount listed in this chapter) is increased each year on January 1. As of 2021, this deductible is $1,484.

2. **YOUR FIRST SIXTY DAYS IN THE HOSPITAL:** After you have reached the benefit period deductible, Medicare covers 100 percent of your inpatient care for the first sixty days that you spend in a hospital. This coverage includes a semiprivate room, meals, general nursing and doctor care, and drugs administered in the hospital. Medicare does not cover a private room (unless a doctor has deemed it medically necessary), private-duty nursing, personal care items such as

slipper socks or razors, or a television or phone in your room if the hospital charges separately for these items.

In addition, it's important to remember that an overnight stay in a hospital does not necessarily mean that you are an inpatient and therefore covered by Medicare. You are only considered an inpatient once a doctor has formally admitted you to the hospital.

3. **DAYS SIXTY-ONE THROUGH NINETY:** If your stay in the hospital stretches past sixty days for a single benefit period, Medicare no longer picks up 100 percent of the tab for your care. For days sixty-one through ninety, you must pay a coinsurance amount, while Medicare pays for the remainder. As of 2021, that coinsurance amount is $371 per day, although the price goes up each year.

4. **RESERVE DAYS:** Once you have spent ninety days in the hospital during a single benefit period, you have reached the end of what Medicare covers. However, you do have what's known as "lifetime reserve days." These are additional days that Medicare will help pay for when you have stayed in the hospital past ninety days during a particular benefit period. Each beneficiary has a total of sixty reserve days to use in his or her lifetime. There is a coinsurance amount— currently set at $742 per reserve day in 2021—which you must pay in order to use your reserve days. You do not have to use all of these reserve days during one benefit period, but once you have used any reserve days, they are gone forever.

5. **MORE THAN 150 DAYS IN THE HOSPITAL:** If you end up staying in the hospital for more than 150 days during a particular benefit period, you have exhausted your Medicare benefits and are on the hook for all medical costs incurred while in the hospital. However, do not forget that once you have been out of the hospital for at least sixty days, a return to the hospital will at that point be considered a different benefit period, meaning that you will again be covered for your care.

Skilled Nursing Facility Care

One common misconception about Medicare is that the program covers a stay in a nursing home. Unfortunately, the reality is that you are covered for only a limited amount of skilled nursing care on an inpatient basis. The operative word here is "skilled." That means that any kind of long-term care you might need that does not require medical knowledge—such as help with daily activities like bathing, dressing, eating, walking, etc.—is not covered by Medicare.

Medicare covers your stay in a skilled nursing facility after you have spent a minimum of three days as an inpatient in the hospital for medically necessary reasons—and the length of your inpatient stay does not include the day that you are discharged. Your doctor must also certify that you need daily skilled care, such as intravenous injections or physical therapy, in order for you to qualify for Medicare benefits.

Medicare covers semiprivate rooms, meals, medically necessary supplies, and nursing and rehabilitative services in a skilled nursing facility. As with hospital coverage, Medicare won't pay for you to have a private room or a telephone or television in your room.

1. **YOUR FIRST TWENTY DAYS IN A SKILLED NURSING FACILITY:** Medicare covers all costs for your first twenty days in such a facility, provided you meet the previously mentioned requirements.

2. **DAYS TWENTY-ONE THROUGH ONE HUNDRED:** After your first twenty days, Medicare requires you to pay a coinsurance amount for each day of your care. As of 2021, that amount is $185.50 per day.

3. **MORE THAN ONE HUNDRED DAYS OF CARE:** After you have stayed for one hundred days in a skilled nursing facility, you have exhausted your Medicare benefits for that benefit period. (As with hospital stays, if you end up having to return to a skilled nursing facility during a different benefit period, Medicare will kick in again and pay for that care.) Unlike Medicare-covered hospital stays, you cannot use reserve days during a stay at a skilled nursing facility, so you must pay for all costs after reaching day one hundred in a benefit period.

Home Healthcare

Things get a little trickier with home healthcare coverage. In short, in order to qualify for such care, you must be homebound, you must have a doctor's order for specific types of healthcare within your home, and you must receive your care from a Medicare-certified home healthcare agency. Those specific types of healthcare that qualify for Medicare coverage include medically necessary skilled nursing care (either part-time or intermittent, but not round-the-clock), physical and occupational therapy, and speech-language or pathology services.

Medicare pays 100 percent of these covered services. However, you will have to pay 20 percent of the Medicare-approved amount for any durable medical equipment (such as walkers, hospital beds, etc.) that you may need for your home healthcare.

MEDICARE-APPROVED AMOUNT

Medicare negotiates with doctors and hospitals regarding the amount of money the program is willing to pay for services and equipment. Doctors who accept the Medicare "assignment" (these doctors are also known as assigned doctors or providers) agree to accept no more than the Medicare-approved amount as payment. That means that a beneficiary using an assigned doctor will only have to pay the deductible and/or coinsurance. However, doctors who are "unassigned" may charge more than the Medicare-approved amount, which means that the Medicare beneficiary may have to pay more than the deductible and/or coinsurance required by Medicare. We will cover this topic in more depth later in this chapter.

Hospice Care

If you need hospice care, Medicare will cover 100 percent of the charges (with two exceptions; see the following explanation). In order to qualify, your doctor must have given you a diagnosis of a terminal illness and a prognosis of six months or less. If you defy the odds, Medicare will continue to cover your hospice care for as long as your doctor feels that the case is terminal. There is no limit to the amount of hospice care that you may receive through Medicare.

Medicare does not pay for your stay in a facility to receive hospice care unless your doctor and hospice team determine that your needs cannot be addressed at home.

The two exceptions to the 100 percent payment rule are for prescription drugs for pain and symptom management that are administered at home, and for respite care. Medicare requires that you pay up to a $5 copayment for each prescription administered at home, and for 5 percent of the Medicare-approved amount for up to five days of inpatient care in order to give your primary caretakers a respite.

Medicare Part B

This is the other half of Original Medicare, and you may hear it referred to as Medicare medical insurance. Unlike Part A, Part B requires all beneficiaries who enroll in it to pay a monthly premium. Part B is intended to help patients pay for the types of medical care and treatment received outside of a hospital. This program covers, in short, services from doctors and other healthcare providers, outpatient care, home healthcare, durable medical equipment, and some preventive care. When coupled with Medicare Part A, Part B can help beneficiaries pay for the majority of medical treatments a senior might need.

THE COST OF MEDICARE PART B

As mentioned previously, the majority of Medicare beneficiaries will pay $148.50 (as of 2021) in monthly premiums for Part B. However, the amount that you pay in premiums is determined by your adjusted gross income as of two years prior. The following Part B premium-pricing chart is reproduced from www.medicare.gov:

Medicare Part B Premium Costs by Income

IF YOUR YEARLY INCOME IN 2019 WAS		YOU PAY
(FILING INDIVIDUAL TAX RETURN)	(FILING JOINT TAX RETURN)	
$88,000 or less	$176,000 or less	$148.50
$88,001 to $111,000	$176,001 to $222,000	$207.90
$111,001 to $138,000	$222,001 to $276,000	$297.00
$138,001 to $165,000	$276,001 to $330,000	$386.10
$165,001 to $500,000	$330,001 to $750,000	$475.20
above $500,000	above $750,000	$504.90

(Please note, all of these figures are accurate as of 2021, but the amounts of both the qualifying adjusted gross incomes and the premium costs are adjusted every year.)

Generally, the cost to receive Medicare coverage for services breaks down as follows: You will pay all costs for services until you meet the yearly deductible, which is currently set at $203 for 2021. Once you have met that deductible, you will typically pay 20 percent of the Medicare-approved amount for any particular service, as long as the healthcare service provider accepts assignment.

Unfortunately, there is no yearly limit on how much you will have to pay out of pocket through Medicare Part B, which is why relying on just Medicare Parts A and B for your health insurance needs can be costly. We will discuss ways to reduce that cost both later in this chapter (in our discussions of Parts C and D), as well as in Chapter 8.

Understanding Medicare Assignment and Medicare-Approved Amounts

As mentioned previously, Medicare negotiates with doctors and healthcare service providers to set prices for particular services, tests, medical goods, etc. The amount agreed upon by both Medicare and the service provider is known as the Medicare-approved amount. Any healthcare that Medicare will cover is based upon that approved amount, which means that a doctor can expect to receive 80 percent of that amount from Medicare for a Medicare patient, while the patient will owe the remaining 20 percent of the Medicare-approved amount to the doctor as coinsurance. Since most doctors who treat Medicare patients accept assignment, paying this coinsurance is what you can expect from the majority of your medical bills.

But what if you see a doctor who does not accept assignment? That's when things get a little complicated. At that point, the doctor may charge you for the difference between the Medicare-approved amount and the full amount that she or he usually charges—up to 15 percent of the Medicare-approved amount. It will be up to you (or your supplemental health insurance, which we will discuss in more depth later) to pay that amount.

In both cases, the doctor is required to accept less money total than she would normally accept from a non-Medicare patient. However, the doctor cannot legally ask for more than 35 percent of the Medicare-approved amount from the patient if the doctor is not assigned. (Also, note that all doctors, whether they are assigned or not, must handle the Medicare billing paperwork gratis, which means you should never be charged for Medicare paperwork processing.)

The issue of Medicare-approved amounts is the reason why you will find some doctors who simply do not accept Medicare patients. In order to keep your healthcare costs low, it pays to make certain that you always see assigned providers.

WHAT DOES MEDICARE PART B COVER?

The good news about Part B for current and soon-to-be retirees is that many preventive medical services are now covered by this Medicare program. New Part B beneficiaries are eligible for a no out-of-pocket cost "Welcome to Medicare" preventive care doctor visit within the first twelve months after signing up. In addition, you are eligible for an annual wellness visit to check on your health and keep you up to date on necessary preventive care. Many preventive treatments, such as flu shots, mammograms, and diabetes screenings, cost nothing out of pocket, provided you go to a doctor or service provider who accepts Medicare assignment. For some preventive services, however, you may still have to pay a deductible, coinsurance, or both.

In addition to the preventive services covered by Medicare Part B, this program also covers most basic medical services, medically necessary outpatient services, laboratory tests, and items that you may need to stay healthy in your golden years. You can find a full list of services covered by Medicare Part B by downloading or requesting the current "Medicare & You" handbook at www.medicare.gov/medicare-you-handbook. You can also check on specific tests, services, and items at www.medicare.gov/coverage.

However, even with Medicare Part B's coverage of preventive services and many types of treatment, there are some big holes in coverage. In particular, this program does not cover:

- Long-term care, also known as custodial care (this is nonmedical help that the elderly might need for daily living)
- Self-administered prescription drugs (i.e., any prescriptions you take at home that you do not need a doctor or nurse to administer)
- Routine dental or eye care
- Dentures
- Cosmetic surgery
- Acupuncture
- Hearing aids and the exams for fitting them
- Routine foot care

These are the most notable exceptions to coverage within Medicare Part B—there are plenty of other services that Original Medicare does not cover. That is why many Medicare beneficiaries will opt into Medicare Parts C and/or D (also known as the Medicare Advantage Plan and Medicare prescription drug coverage, respectively) to help ensure that they are fully covered. We will discuss these two optional additions to Medicare presently, but first, let's look at the enrollment requirements for Original Medicare.

Enrolling in Original Medicare

The rules about enrolling in Medicare vary depending on your circumstances. Unfortunately, missing an enrollment deadline can be costly, so it's important to make sure you're aware of what you need to do to sign up for Medicare Parts A and B.

AUTOMATIC ENROLLMENT

Some Medicare beneficiaries will be automatically enrolled in the program without having to lift a finger. There are three reasons why you might find yourself receiving a Medicare Part A and Part B card in the mail without enrolling:

1. You are already receiving Social Security benefits or Railroad Retirement Board benefits. For these individuals, Medicare Parts A and B will automatically kick in on the first day of the month they turn sixty-five—unless their birthday is on the first of the month, in which case their benefits begin on the first day of the month prior to their sixty-fifth birthday.
2. You are under sixty-five, disabled, and have been receiving Social Security disability benefits for twenty-four months. At that point, you become automatically eligible and enrolled for Medicare Parts A and B.
3. You have ALS (amyotrophic lateral sclerosis, also known as Lou Gehrig's disease). You will be automatically enrolled in Medicare Parts A and B in the same month that your Social Security disability benefits begin.

As you'll recall, however, Medicare Part B is not premium-free, which means being automatically enrolled in Medicare in this way requires you to start paying the monthly premiums. While most seniors will find it is to their financial benefit to enroll in Medicare Part B, you may decide that you do not want to take part in that program, even if you are automatically enrolled in it.

Beneficiaries who are automatically enrolled receive their Medicare card in the mail three months before their sixty-fifth birthday, or one month before their twenty-fifth month of Social Security disability benefits. On the back of the card are instructions for declining Part B coverage. Those who decline will need to follow those instructions and return the Medicare card in the mail to avoid being charged for the Part B premiums.

SIGNING UP FOR PART A AND PART B

If you are nearing your sixty-fifth birthday and you have not started receiving Social Security retirement benefits or been on Social Security disability, then you will have to sign up for benefits yourself. The following are the three time frames during which you may sign up for Medicare Parts A and B:

THE INITIAL ENROLLMENT PERIOD

This is the best time to enroll in Medicare. The initial enrollment period is a seven-month time frame that begins three months before the month you turn sixty-five, includes the month you turn sixty-five, and ends three months after the month you turn sixty-five. If you enroll in Medicare Parts A and/or B during this enrollment period, then there is no fee or penalty for enrollment. Enrolling during the three months before your sixty-fifth birthday means that you will have Medicare coverage starting on the first day of your birthday month. If you enroll during your birthday month, or in the three months that follow, you will have a delayed start date for coverage. So it's best to get the ball rolling with Medicare before your sixty-fifth birthday.

THE GENERAL ENROLLMENT PERIOD

If you missed the seven-month initial enrollment period window, you can still sign up. There is a general enrollment period between January 1 and March 31 every year. Signing up during general enrollment means that your coverage will begin July 1 of that year. However, there is a penalty for missing your initial enrollment period.

For Part A, if you are not eligible for the premium-free program and you do not sign up for Part A during your initial enrollment period, your monthly premium will increase by 10 percent for each twelve-month period that you could have had Part A but didn't sign up. You will pay this penalty for twice the number of years that you neglected to sign up. (For instance, if you waited one year, you would pay the 10 percent premium increase for two years.) It's important to note, however, that if you are eligible for premium-free Part A, there is no penalty for late enrollment.

If you miss the initial enrollment period for Part B, the financial consequences are more severe. As with Part A, the monthly premium will increase by 10 percent for each full twelve-month period that you were eligible for Part B but did not sign up. However, you will have to pay the late enrollment penalty for as long as you are a Medicare beneficiary.

THE SPECIAL ENROLLMENT PERIOD

This period is for those beneficiaries who were covered under a group health plan through either their own or their spouse's employment when they turned sixty-five. Those potential beneficiaries who already have health insurance as of their sixty-fifth birthday are not required to sign up for Medicare during their initial enrollment period.

Medicare will allow such double-covered beneficiaries to enroll at any time when they are still covered by their group health plan or during the eight-month period that begins the month after either the employment or the health coverage ends—whichever happens first.

Medicare Advantage and Medicare Prescription Drug Coverage

While Original Medicare covers many of the healthcare costs you may face in retirement, it is by no means a complete healthcare coverage system. This is why Medicare also offers two more optional programs: Part C, or the Medicare Advantage Plan, which is offered to Medicare beneficiaries by Medicare-approved private insurance companies, and Part D, the prescription drug plan.

Unfortunately, since Part C plans are offered through private insurance companies, and the Part D coverage plan has some serious financial gaps in it, both of these additions to Medicare can be rather tough to figure out. Here's what you need to know about Medicare Parts C and D.

MEDICARE PART C

If you opt to join a Medicare Advantage Plan (or Part C), you are in effect getting all of your Medicare insurance—including the hospital and medical insurance included in Medicare Parts A and B—through a private insurer. The good news is that you will only have to deal with a single insurer and set of paperwork in order to handle your medical bills. The bad news is that there are any number of insurers who offer Medicare Advantage Plans, so it is very difficult to generalize about what to expect from these plans.

There are several different types of Advantage Plans:

- **HEALTH MAINTENANCE ORGANIZATION (HMO) PLANS:** These plans will allow you to only go to healthcare providers, hospitals, and doctors that are within the plan's network. HMOs also will often require referrals from primary care physicians in order to schedule an appointment with a new doctor.

- **PREFERRED PROVIDER ORGANIZATION (PPO) PLANS:** Like HMOs, PPOs have a list of providers within their network, but these are preferred, rather than required, providers. You will pay less by staying in-network, but your claim will not be refused if you go out of network.

- **PRIVATE FEE-FOR-SERVICE (PFFS) PLANS:** With a PFFS plan, you may see any healthcare provider who agrees to treat you—much like how Original Medicare works. The plan decides how much insurance will pay for services and how much of the remainder you are responsible for.

- **SPECIAL NEEDS PLAN (SNP):** These plans offer focused and specialized healthcare for particular groups of individuals, like those who are both Medicare and Medicaid beneficiaries, those who live in a nursing home, or those suffering from certain chronic conditions.

- **HMO POINT-OF-SERVICE PLANS:** Like traditional HMOs, these plans have a network of doctors that you may see. However, you may be able to get some care from providers who are out of network by paying a higher copayment or coinsurance.

- **MEDICARE MEDICAL SAVINGS ACCOUNT (MSA) PLANS:** MSA plans combine a high-deductible healthcare plan with a bank account. Medicare will deposit money (minus your yearly deductible) into your account, which you can use to pay for healthcare throughout the year.

Deciding which Medicare Advantage Plan is right for you can be a difficult prospect. It pays to shop around and crunch the numbers. Medicare offers a plan finder tool that can help you make your decision (www.medicare.gov/plan-compare).

THE COST OF MEDICARE PART C

Since each plan will offer different premiums, care options, deductibles, copayments, and coinsurance, it is impossible to generalize how much you will be paying out of pocket for a Medicare Advantage Plan. However, it's important to note that Medicare Advantage Plans cannot charge you more than Original Medicare does for certain services, including chemotherapy, dialysis, and skilled nursing facility care. In addition, these types of plans also have yearly caps on how much you pay for Part A and Part B services each year, although those out-of-pocket caps can differ between Medicare Advantage Plans and are subject to change from year to year.

WHAT DOES MEDICARE PART C COVER?

Again, each specific plan will have its own list of covered services, so that is one of the important factors to consider while deciding between

Medicare Advantage Plans. Most of these plans include prescription drug coverage, however, so if you decide to go this route, your Medicare Advantage experience will be similar to the types of comprehensive health insurance plans you were used to through your employer before retirement.

JOINING A MEDICARE PART C PLAN

A benefit of signing up for a Medicare Advantage Plan is that you have a great deal of flexibility. You may sign up during your initial enrollment period for Original Medicare or during the open enrollment period between October 15 and December 7 each year. In order to be eligible for a Medicare Advantage Plan, you must have (or be enrolling in) Medicare Parts A and B and live within the plan's service area.

According to the "Medicare & You" handbook:

- You can join a Medicare Advantage Plan even if you have a preexisting condition.

- You can join or leave a plan at the following times during the year: Open enrollment, which falls between October 15 and December 7 each year, during which time any eligible beneficiary can join, switch, or drop a Medicare Advantage Plan. This is the only time you can switch to a Medicare Advantage Plan from Original Medicare. Your coverage will begin on January 1.

- Between January 1 and March 31, you may leave your Medicare Advantage Plan to switch to a different Medicare Advantage Plan or to return to Original Medicare, even if you missed the open enrollment period. However, you cannot enroll in a Medicare Advantage Plan for the first time during this enrollment period. Your new coverage will begin on the first day of the month after the plan receives your enrollment request.

- Each year, Medicare Advantage Plans can choose to leave Medicare or make changes to the services they cover and what you pay. You have the opportunity and the right to leave or change plans if that occurs.

You are generally required to stay enrolled in your Medicare Advantage Plan for an entire calendar year, starting with the date your coverage begins. But even this requirement allows for a great deal of flexibility should you decide you're unhappy with your Medicare Advantage Plan provider.

Medicare Part D

This prescription drug plan has only been in place since 2006. It was created in order to help seniors who are only using Original Medicare to pay for their prescription drugs, since neither Part A nor Part B cover self-administered prescriptions. If you have enrolled in a Medicare Advantage Plan, you will likely already have prescription drug coverage as part of your plan. It only makes sense to enroll in Medicare Part D if you are only using Original Medicare.

THE COST OF MEDICARE PART D

Like Medicare Advantage Plans, the prescription drug plans (sometimes called PDPs) are administered by private insurance companies, which means that costs vary from plan to plan. The specific monthly premiums, yearly deductible, and coinsurance or copay amounts will be different depending upon which plan you choose. However, every Medicare Prescription Drug Plan follows these four phases:

- **DEDUCTIBLE PERIOD:** Until you have met your deductible, you will be responsible for the full negotiated price for your prescription drugs. Each plan's deductible is set by the insurer, and some plans have no deductible at all. However, Medicare specifies that no plan can have a deductible greater than $445 in 2021.

- **INITIAL COVERAGE PERIOD:** Once you have met your deductible (if your plan has one), your Medicare Prescription Drug Plan will help pay for your covered prescriptions. You will be required to pay a copay or coinsurance amount, and the plan will pay for anything above that amount. The initial coverage period ends after you reach a certain dollar amount spent on prescriptions. In 2021, that dollar limit is $4,130.

- **COVERAGE GAP:** After your total annual drug costs have passed the $4,130 limit (as of 2021), you enter the coverage gap. In the coverage gap, you become responsible for 25 percent of the cost of your drugs. For instance, let's say your coinsurance amount is $20. Once you have reached the coverage gap, if your prescription drug's total cost is $200, you will have to pay $50 for it, rather than the $20 coinsurance amount you paid for the same drug during the initial coverage period.

- **CATASTROPHIC COVERAGE PERIOD:** After you have reached the coverage gap, your drug costs can go down again if you reach the catastrophic coverage dollar amount in out-of-pocket spending. As of 2021, that catastrophic coverage amount is set at $6,550. Once you reach the catastrophic coverage period, you are only expected to pay a small copay or coinsurance for any future prescription costs.

WHAT COUNTS TOWARD OUT-OF-POCKET COSTS?

The following costs are included in the calculation to help you get out of the coverage gap and reach the catastrophic coverage for Medicare Prescription Drug Plans:

- Your annual deductible
- The coinsurance and/or copays you paid during the initial coverage period
- The 25 percent out-of-pocket amounts you paid during the coverage gap
- The discount you received on brand-name drugs while in the coverage gap

However, not all drug costs can help you get out of the coverage gap. These costs do not count toward the catastrophic coverage minimum:

- The premium you pay for Medicare Part D
- Pharmacy dispensing fees
- The cost of drugs that are not covered by your Medicare Part D plan

JOINING A MEDICARE PART D PRESCRIPTION DRUG PLAN

As with Original Medicare, it is important to join a Medicare Part D plan during the seven months of your initial enrollment period. If you join a prescription drug plan after the end of the eligibility period, or if you let your prescription drug coverage lapse for more than sixty-three days, then you will be subject to a late-enrollment penalty.

While it is important to sign up for your prescription drug coverage during your initial enrollment period, there are open enrollment periods every year. These, like the Medicare Advantage enrollment, are between October 15 and December 7 of each year, with an effective date for coverage of January 1.

You can also switch Medicare prescription drug coverage carriers during any open enrollment period, and you do not have to cancel your old Medicare drug plan when you switch to a new one. The old one will end when your new coverage begins.

As with Medicare Advantage, you will generally have to stay with your prescription drug plan for an entire calendar year before you may switch or drop coverage.

CHAPTER 7 TAKEAWAYS

☑ While the future of healthcare in America is almost anybody's guess, traditional Medicare will likely maintain its current shape and stability over the coming years, even if details change.

☑ Medicare Part A is premium-free for the majority of Americans and (partially) covers inpatient hospital care, inpatient care in a skilled nursing facility, home healthcare, and hospice care.

☑ After you have met your deductible, Medicare Part A covers 100 percent of your first sixty days of an inpatient stay in a hospital. After sixty days, Medicare Part A continues to offer partial coverage of your stay up to a limit.

☑ Most beneficiaries pay a $148.50 monthly premium for Medicare Part B as of 2021, although those with high incomes pay higher premiums, and the monthly premium is adjusted each year.

☑ Medicare Part B covers both treatment and preventive care. In general, you can expect to pay 20 percent of the Medicare-approved amount for services with Medicare-assigned doctors and healthcare providers.

☑ Enrolling in Original Medicare (comprising Parts A and B) during your initial enrollment period ensures you will not pay a late-enrollment penalty. The initial enrollment period is the seven-month period that includes the three months prior to your sixty-fifth birthday month, the month of your sixty-fifth birthday, and the three months after your sixty-fifth birthday.

☑ Medicare Part C (also known as Medicare Advantage Plan) provides you with all of your Medicare insurance, including Parts A and B, through a private insurer. Medicare Advantage Plan costs vary from provider to provider.

☑ You may join a Medicare Advantage Plan even if you have a pre-existing condition. You are eligible to enroll in these plans during your initial enrollment period for Original Medicare, and between October 15 and December 7 each year. You may switch or drop plans between January 1 and March 15 each year, but you cannot enroll in a Medicare Advantage Plan for the first time during that period.

☑ Medicare Part D is a prescription drug insurance that is administered by private insurers. You will pay a coinsurance amount for your prescription drugs with a Medicare Part D plan, until you have reached a total drug cost of $4,130 for the year (as of 2021). At that point, you will pay 25 percent of your total drug costs, until you have reached an out-of-pocket spending limit of $6,550 for the year (as of 2021). After that, you will only pay a small coinsurance amount for each prescription until the end of the year.

What to Do When

YOUR AGE	WHAT TO DO
Sixty-four and nine months	Enroll in Medicare Parts A and B. The initial enrollment period for Medicare covers the three months prior to your sixty-fifth birthday, the month of your birthday, and the three following months.
Sixty-four and nine months	If you choose to enroll in a Medicare Advantage Plan and/or a Medicare Prescription Drug Plan, do so at the same time you enroll in Parts A and B.

CHAPTER 8

Planning for Healthcare Expenses in Retirement

WHAT YOU'LL LEARN IN THIS CHAPTER

Healthcare is likely to be one of your largest expenses in retirement, even with the help of Medicare. Unfortunately, the cost of healthcare often takes retirees by surprise, which can make for some very difficult financial decisions. This chapter will help you understand your various healthcare options before you need them. By the end of this chapter, you will know what to expect from healthcare, both before and after you qualify for Medicare, and you will learn strategies you can employ to reduce the bite that healthcare will take out of your nest egg.

In a perfect world, retirement planning would focus entirely on the fun ways you could spend your money (and your time) in your golden years. There would be no need to worry about or budget for health insurance premiums, doctor's visits, medical copays, or hospital stays. In the current financial reality, however, pre-retirees must plan ahead for their healthcare expenses.

That's because healthcare expenses in retirement can be staggering. Each year, Fidelity calculates the average cost of medical care for a sixty-five-year-old couple retiring during that calendar year. For 2020, Fidelity calculated that the average couple would need $295,000 in today's dollars to cover their medical expenses for the rest of their lives. Not only does this calculation not include the cost of long-term care (which we'll discuss more later in the chapter); it also assumes that the couple are both on Medicare. In fact, Medicare premiums make up 39 percent, or $115,050, of Fidelity's calculation. (The remaining breakdown is 43 percent to copayments, coinsurance, and deductibles, and 18 percent to prescription drugs.)

If these numbers weren't upsetting enough, it's also important to note that Fidelity's estimates have risen almost every year. The 2020 estimate of $295,000 is a 3.5 percent increase over the 2019 estimate of $285,000, and an 84.4 percent increase over the 2002 estimate of $160,000. In short, it's quite likely that your medical expenses in retirement will cost a pretty penny.

Before you start breathing into a paper bag, there are a couple of important things to remember about the annual Fidelity calculations: First, these calculations assume that bad health only worsens with age and will necessarily lead to less independence. For instance, the Fidelity numbers assume that once a retiree breaks a hip, he will need consistent (or increasing) inpatient medical care for the rest of his life. However, in most cases, your need for healthcare will wax and wane throughout your retirement. If you do break a hip (perish the thought!), it's likely you will need inpatient medical care while you recover, but you will be able to eventually return home and resume your normal life. This type of improvement makes healthcare much more difficult to calculate, but it also means your costs are likely to fluctuate.

In addition, taking better care of yourself can help to improve your health and potentially reduce the need for medical care as you age. Adequate sleep, exercise, and healthy eating may not seem like part of your financial plan, but they can potentially have a greater return than any traditional investment. That said, even the most fit ultramarathoner who consumes only kale smoothies is not immune to the vagaries of poor health. But you will never regret taking care of yourself, because at the very least, it helps you feel better in the present.

Of course, even the reassuring understanding that you will not necessarily spend $295,000 in medical care in retirement doesn't help you plan for those costs. That's where the following strategies come in:

Medicare Supplement Insurance, aka Medigap

Medicare Supplement Insurance, more commonly known as Medigap insurance, is private health insurance designed to help you fill the "gaps" in Original Medicare coverage. Your Medigap policy will help you pay for some of the costs that Medicare does not cover, including deductibles, copayments, and coinsurance. Medigap is not like Medicare Advantage, because the Medicare Advantage Plans provide you with ways to get your Medicare benefits, whereas Medigap works as a supplement to your Original Medicare benefits. That means that if you have a Medicare Advantage Plan, you do not need, and cannot legally be sold, a Medigap policy.

WHAT DOES MEDIGAP COVER?

For the most part, Medigap helps you with the copayments and coinsurance that you must pay when using Original Medicare. When you visit the doctor or otherwise make a health claim through Medicare while you are covered by Medigap insurance, Medicare will pay its portion of the Medicare-approved amount (see Chapter 7), and Medigap will pay its own portion. Anything that remains is your responsibility. Until January 1, 2020, some Medigap plans covered the deductible for Medicare Part B. However, as of January 1, 2020, Medigap plans sold to new Medicare beneficiaries are no longer allowed to cover the Part B deductible. This means Medigap Plans C and F will no longer be available to new Medicare beneficiaries.

There are currently ten different types of Medigap policies, and private insurers must clearly identify which policy you are purchasing and label it as Medicare supplement insurance. The policies are generally identified by letters A through N, and all policies with the same letter designation offer the same basic benefits. That will make it easier for potential beneficiaries to compare policies to determine the best fit for their needs.

MEDIGAP PLANS E, H, I, AND J

If you're scratching your head over why ten policies would need fourteen letter designations, that's because four plan types—E, H, I, and J—are no longer offered.

You can expect each of the ten available policies to cover the following percentage of various benefits:

Medicare Supplement Insurance (Medigap) Benefits Plan

BENEFITS	A	B	C	D	F*	G*	K	L	M	N
Medicare Part A coinsurance and hospital costs (up to an additional 365 days after Medicare benefits are used)	100%	100%	100%	100%	100%	100%	100%	100%	100%	100%
Medicare Part B coinsurance or copayment	100%	100%	100%	100%	100%	100%	50%	75%	100%	100%†
Blood (first 3 pints)	100%	100%	100%	100%	100%	100%	50%	75%	100%	100%
Part A hospice care coinsurance or copayment	100%	100%	100%	100%	100%	100%	50%	75%	100%	100%
Skilled nursing facility care coinsurance	0%	0%	100%	100%	100%	100%	50%	75%	100%	100%
Medicare Part A deductible	0%	100%	100%	100%	100%	100%	50%	75%	50%	100%
Medicare Part B deductible**	0%	0%	100%	0%	100%	0%	0%	0%	0%	0%
Medicare Part B excess charges	0%	0%	0%	0%	100%	100%	0%	0%	0%	0%
Foreign travel emergency (up to plan limits) ††	0%	0%	80%	80%	80%	100%	0%	0%	80%	80%
Out-of-pocket limit	N/A	N/A	N/A	N/A	N/A	N/A	$6,220 as of 2021	$3,110 as of 2021	N/A	N/A

*Plans F and G also offer a high-deductible plan with a deductible of $2,370 (as of 2021). Once you have met this deductible, Medigap pays 100 percent of covered services for the rest of the year. The high-deductible Plan F is not available to anyone who becomes eligible for Medicare on January 1, 2020, or later.

†For Plan N, the policy will pay 100 percent of Part B coinsurance except for a copayment of up to $20 for some office visits and a copayment of up to $50 for emergency room visits.

**Plans C and F (that pay the Medicare Part B deductible) will not be available to anyone who becomes eligible for Medicare on January 1, 2020, or later.

††Please note that Original Medicare does not cover any foreign travel emergencies.

(Chart courtesy of www.medicare.gov/supplements-other-insurance/how-to-compare-medigap-policies)

While Medigap policies can help bridge the gap between the limits of Original Medicare coverage and what you are personally responsible for, it's important to remember that there are still some areas of coverage you cannot count on with a Medigap policy. In particular, Medigap does not cover long-term care (as in the type of nonmedical care you might need if you are unable to care for yourself), vision care, dental care, hearing aids, eyeglasses, or private nursing. It's a good idea to plan for these costs in retirement. Later in this chapter, we'll discuss an option for long-term care that can help reduce your potential healthcare costs. One last benefit that you cannot count on from Medigap is prescription drug coverage. Therefore, if you intend to enroll in a Medigap insurance plan, it's a good idea to pair it with a Medicare Part D prescription drug program.

ENROLLING IN A MEDIGAP PLAN

To be eligible for a Medigap policy, you must be enrolled in both Medicare Part A and Part B. The best time to enroll in a Medigap plan is during your particular Medigap open enrollment period, which is the six-month span starting on the first day of the month in which you are sixty-five or older and enrolled in Medicare Part B. For example, if you wait to enroll in Medicare Part B until a year after you have turned sixty-five, your Medigap open enrollment period begins on the first day of the month you are enrolled in Part B coverage, even though you are already older than sixty-five.

If you enroll in a Medigap program during that time period, then you will be allowed to purchase any Medigap policy the insurer offers, no matter the state of your health, at the same price that healthy purchasers pay. If you miss the open enrollment deadline, Medigap insurers are allowed to use medical underwriting to determine whether they will insure you and how much they will charge you.

It's also important to remember that you must purchase Medigap individually. These policies only cover one person, so spouses cannot purchase their Medigap insurance together.

THE AVERAGE COST OF MEDIGAP POLICIES

Since the policies and prices for premiums vary from plan to plan, insurer to insurer, and state to state, it's difficult to say with confidence exactly how much you can expect to pay for your Medigap insurance policy. Rates also vary depending on where you live. In 2018, cost for Medigap Plan G ranged from $116 to $134 per month in Texas, while the cost for the same Medigap Plan G ranged from $255 to $300 per month in Florida. Retirees will need to carefully weigh the options between Medicare Part C (i.e., Medicare Advantage Plans) and the various Medigap policies to decide which will ultimately be the most affordable.

Other Insurance Issues to Consider

Any discussion of healthcare is incomplete without a look at the sorts of coverage that health insurance does not provide. In particular, disability coverage and long-term care coverage are big holes in both private health insurance and Medicare benefits. In order to keep your nest egg in good health, you will need to factor in the possibility that you may become disabled before retirement or that you may need long-term nonmedical care as you age.

Disability Insurance

We tend to think that most disabilities arise from accidents, but in fact illness is behind the majority of long-term absences from work. Finding yourself unable to work in the last five years before you reach retirement could seriously derail your plans.

The other common misconception about disability, particularly among those nearing retirement age, is that Social Security disability benefits are available should you become disabled during this critical time. Unfortunately, that is not necessarily the case. The requirements for eligibility for Social Security disability benefits are stringent. For instance, Social Security needs to determine that you are not only unable to perform your own job but that you are also unable to perform any job that might be related to your field of expertise and education. While the SSA does not ask disabled workers to take any old job (like burger flipper or Walmart greeter) if they're no longer able to continue in their career, the requirements make it extremely difficult to qualify for disability benefits. In addition, your condition must either have lasted or be expected to last for at least one year, or your condition must be expected to result in your death. The long and short of it is that you should not count on Social Security disability should you come down with pneumonia or get into a bad car accident. It is better to get adequate disability coverage to insure your last few years of working.

WHAT DISABILITY INSURANCE GENERALLY COVERS

Most disability policies will cover 60 percent of your lost income. While you can purchase additional policies that increase that percentage, be aware that there are no insurers that will replace 100 percent of your income. (Otherwise, what incentive would you have to get back to work?) Disability policies also come in two flavors: "own occupation" and "any occupation." Own occupation policies cover you if your disability keeps you from doing the job for which you are trained—even if you could potentially get another job doing something less demanding. Any occupation policies, on the other hand, will only cover you if you're unable to handle any job, no matter how simple or menial. That's problematic because even if your traumatic brain injury ends your career as a lawyer, you may still be able to hold down a job cleaning offices—for a tiny fraction of the pay you were used to as an attorney.

Any occupation coverage tends to be cheaper to purchase, for obvious reasons, but it's smart to spend the extra money on an own occupation policy. Otherwise, you might find that a disability changes not only your health but also your financial life.

Finally, you should note that some own occupation policies become any occupation coverage after a period of time (typically two years). In theory, these policies give you the time to train for another job, but for many, it could just mean loss of coverage after two years.

THE COST OF DISABILITY INSURANCE

Unfortunately, disability insurance doesn't come cheap, and unlike life insurance, there is not an enormous marketplace of providers. In addition, the older you are when you purchase disability coverage, the more it will cost you. If you have never had coverage prior to being five years away from retirement, you may find that premiums are priced prohibitively.

So how much can you expect to pay? In general, long-term, comprehensive disability insurance will cost around 1 to 4 percent of your annual pre-tax income. Which means that if you make $100,000 per year, you can expect to pay between $1,000 and $4,000 per year for your disability insurance premiums. However, premiums increase with age, which means you are likely to pay closer to 4 percent (or more). In addition, women can generally expect to pay 20 to 60 percent more for disability insurance than men do. This is because women are more likely to make disability claims.

It is possible to reduce the cost burden of premiums by increasing the elimination period—that is, the waiting period before you start receiving benefits—from the typical span of ninety days to a much less expensive option of 180 days. Underwriting for disability insurance is also quite onerous, since the insurer will examine your health, your age, your occupation, and your finances.

However, if your employer offers disability insurance, you can take advantage of the lower cost of joining a group policy, and in most cases avoid the medical underwriting process in order to qualify. However, employer-sponsored disability insurance is often insufficient. It may offer the bare minimum of income replacement, only be valid for a short term (which is admittedly less of a concern for someone within five years of retirement), or have long waiting periods before benefits kick in. Considering that you are currently in your peak earning years and are using your income for both living expenses and retirement savings, it is worth your while to look into supplemental disability insurance even if you are insured through your employer. Supplemental policies can be easier to obtain than individual policies, and this can help you rest easy, knowing that your nest egg and your life are safe should you become temporarily or permanently disabled.

If you cannot get disability insurance through your employer, you should still look into purchasing an individual policy. While your age may make you ineligible for anything but the most expensive of disability policies—most insurers will not offer disability policies once you reach age sixty—take the time to crunch the numbers with your trusted financial adviser to see which risk makes the most sense: risk being uninsured and having to dip into your savings should you become disabled in the next five years, or risk the additional cost of potentially unused premiums while you're gearing up for retirement.

Long-Term Care Insurance

While disability insurance can help protect you before you retire, an even more problematic gap in your insurance coverage is what you will do if you need long-term care after you retire. According to the US Department of Health and Human Services, someone who turns sixty-five today has an almost 70 percent chance of needing some sort of long-term care service. While one-third of current sixty-five-year-olds may not need any long-term care as they age, 20 percent will need long-term care for longer than five years. Neither Medicare nor private health insurance covers the sort of nonmedical daily living care that many elderly individuals need—which includes help with eating, bathing, dressing, and mobility.

While our parents and grandparents might have been able to get around this problem by having Great-Grandpa move in with a member of the family, that's not nearly as feasible in a world where fewer young adults stay in the same spot where they were born and raised and dual-income marriages are now the norm. Instead of planning to have your children take care of you, you're much more likely to need in-home care, adult daycare, or even a nursing home.

If that prospect isn't unappealing enough, the cost of these different types of care can be staggering. The Department of Health and Human Services reports that as of 2016, the average daily cost for nursing home care is $225. The average nursing home stay lasts 272 days, which comes to a cost of $61,200 for an average stay ($225 × 272 days = $61,200). In-home nursing, while less expensive, can still cost $20.50 per hour of care. Clearly, that could put an enormous dent in your nest egg. Add the fact that some individuals who need long-term care—such as those afflicted with dementia or Alzheimer's—are otherwise perfectly healthy and could live a long life while still needing daily assistance, and the financial prospects are even grimmer.

So other than protecting your health as best you can, what are your options for paying for long-term care? In general, wealthy individuals can afford to pay out of pocket for their long-term care needs. Those with limited assets are eligible for Medicaid, which does pay for long-term care—but limited assets means *limited*. The person needing care cannot have more than $2,000 in his or her own name. Most middle-income retirees would have to completely exhaust their own resources before qualifying for help from Medicaid. (And no transferring your assets to a loved one in order to meet the poverty guidelines—the government is onto that.)

For those in the middle, long-term care insurance may be a savvy way to protect your nest egg.

MY CHANGING VIEW OF LONG-TERM CARE INSURANCE

If you have read either the first edition of this book or any of my other writing from about the same time, you may have noticed that my attitude toward long-term care insurance has shifted from enthusiastic to lukewarm.

Here's why I changed my mind. In 2014, the Center for Retirement Research at Boston College found that previous studies of long-term care usage overstated the duration of care necessary for those who require it. The Center's analysis found that long-term care insurance is optimal for only about 20 to 30 percent of retirees. That means many of my readers will not necessarily be better off with long-term care insurance.

To determine if long-term care insurance is right for you, consider both your health prognosis in retirement and the cost of monthly premiums. If you can reasonably expect decent health in retirement and if long-term care insurance premiums would take a painful bite out of your budget, then you may find it more efficient to save money in a Roth IRA or Health Savings Account instead, which we'll cover later in this chapter.

HOW LONG-TERM CARE INSURANCE WORKS

Unlike health insurance, where the insurance company directly pays the caregiver, long-term care insurance generally requires that the policy holder pay out of pocket for the care, then submit proof of service in order to be reimbursed. In addition, there is usually an elimination period that can span anywhere from twenty to 120 days. This is one way you can save money on premiums: The longer your elimination period, the lower your premiums.

The conventional wisdom about this kind of insurance is that you should purchase it early—in your forties or fifties—in order to "lock in" lower premium rates. However, the promise of locked-in rates is not necessarily binding. While the insurance company cannot raise your individual rate, it can raise the rate of blocks of policyholders, which it generally does as those individuals age and become more likely to file a claim. This means that purchasing the insurance when you are younger makes it more likely that you will see a rate hike before you need the coverage, even though the premiums will be relatively affordable for those first years.

If you are still in good health, purchasing long-term care insurance in the last years before you retire can be perfect timing. While the premiums may be more expensive than they were in your forties, you will be in a better position to afford them and will be less vulnerable to a rate hike.

THE COST OF LONG-TERM CARE INSURANCE

Unfortunately, this type of insurance will cost you. According to the American Association for Long-Term Care Insurance, in 2018, the average cost to insure a sixty-year-old couple was $3,490 combined, with a benefit of $164,000 each.

There are ways to reduce the costs of long-term care insurance. For instance, while it is possible to purchase a long-term care insurance policy that covers any contingency, those premiums will often be out of reach for the average retiree. Instead, choose the policy that will best protect you—and make plans with that policy in mind.

In particular, increasing the elimination period can make your premiums more affordable. However, you will need to know how you can pay for that gap in coverage. Consider having an emergency fund set aside specifically for long-term care.

In addition, lowering your benefits can help to keep your policy affordable. For instance, the typical length of a nursing home stay is less than three years. Many policyholders will opt for the insurance that only covers up to three years' worth of nursing home care, rather than an indefinite stay, in order to save on their premiums.

There are, however, two features that you should make sure are included in your policy. The first is inflation protection, which will ensure that the care you are buying for yourself now will keep pace with rising healthcare costs. The second is a waiver-of-premium benefit, which will allow you to suspend your premium payments once you are eligible for benefits. No matter what type of long-term care insurance you choose, it is generally better to buy before you retire. Costs go up the longer you wait, and poor health can make you ineligible for the insurance. This is another complex decision that your trusted financial adviser can help you to make.

Steps to Take Before Retirement to Keep Your Finances Healthy

Even if you have been diligently saving for retirement for years, you may be frightened of the financial pitfalls of healthcare in retirement. Remember, though, that there is still a great deal you can do over the next five years to save money for your healthcare costs in retirement.

Using a Health Savings Account for Retirement Healthcare Savings

Health Savings Accounts (HSAs) are similar to traditional IRAs, in that contributions up to the legal limit are 100 percent tax-deductible, and the money in the HSA grows tax-deferred. In addition, withdrawals you make in order to pay for qualified medical expenses are not taxed at all—not even earned interest, as long as it is used for medical expenses. Unlike Flexible Spending Accounts, you do not have to use the money in your HSA within a year or risk forfeiting it. The money in your HSA is yours to keep.

In addition, while you cannot make nonmedical withdrawals from an HSA prior to age sixty-five without incurring a 20 percent tax penalty and income tax, any nonmedical withdrawals made after age sixty-five are penalty-free (but still subject to income tax).

But, as long as you use your HSA funds for qualified medical expenses, which include deductibles, copayment, coinsurance, and any care that is not covered by your health insurance, then your money is entirely tax-free. You fund the HSA with pre-tax dollars, pay no taxes on HSA fund growth, and pay no taxes when you withdraw funds for your medical expenses.

Like IRAs, HSAs have contribution limits with catch-up provisions for individuals who are fifty-five or older. Table 8–1 outlines the limits for 2021:

TABLE 8–1:

HSA Contribution Limits in 2021

	CONTRIBUTION LIMIT	55+ CATCH-UP CONTRIBUTION
Single	$3,600	$1,000
Family	$7,200	$1,000

WHAT ARE QUALIFIED MEDICAL EXPENSES FOR HSA WITHDRAWALS?

Nearly all medical expenses that are paid in order to alleviate or prevent illness or defect (including dental and vision expenses) are considered qualified medical expenses for withdrawal from your HSA. However, there are some expenses that are not covered. These include:

- Surgery made solely for cosmetic reasons
- Health club dues
- Illegal operations/treatments
- Maternity clothes
- Toiletries
- Health insurance premiums
- Disability insurance premiums

Long-term care, dental, and vision insurance premiums, as well as health insurance deductibles, are all considered qualified medical expenses, and you can use your HSA to pay for them. In addition, once you are sixty-five and enrolled in Medicare, you may use HSA funds to pay any Medicare insurance premiums, including the premiums for Medicare Part B or for a Medicare Advantage Plan. You may not, however, use your HSA funds to pay for a Medigap policy.

For a complete list of qualified medical expenses, consult IRS Code Section 213(d).

Theoretically, if you and your spouse are over age fifty-five, you could put away $8,200 per year toward future medical expenses, which can really help ensure your financial security in retirement. However, before you start asking where to sign up, it is important to remember that there are some caveats to all that good news. Health Savings Accounts are not for everyone, and for good reason.

HOW DOES A HEALTH SAVINGS ACCOUNT WORK?

In order to be eligible for a Health Savings Account, you must be signed up for a high-deductible health plan (HDHP) and have no other health insurance coverage. (This restriction on other health insurance coverage does not include disability and long-term care insurance.) In 2021, the minimum deductible for an HDHP to qualify for a Health Savings Account is $1,400 for an individual and $2,800 for a family. (Remember, these are the minimums required by the government for an HDHP to be eligible for a Health Savings Account. You may find plans with higher deductibles.) With HDHP healthcare, you must meet the entire deductible for the calendar year before the insurance kicks in. While some high-deductible plans will pay for 100 percent of your covered expenses once the deductible is met, most do not. In 2021, the government has set the maximum out-of-pocket expenses for an HDHP for a single participant at $7,000 and at $14,000 for a family. What that means is as an individual insured with an HDHP, you must pay all expenses out of pocket until you reach the deductible of $1,400, then pay a percentage of any remaining medical expenses until you hit the $7,000 cap, at which point the insurer will pay all further expenses.

You will be paying the (admittedly low) premiums for your HDHP, plus the deductible, plus uncovered medical expenses, plus any copayments or coinsurance required by your plan once you have met the deductible until you reach the spending cap. In addition, you will be contributing to your HSA in the hopes of handling future medical costs, and this option can be expensive, indeed.

WHO SHOULD CHOOSE A HEALTH SAVINGS ACCOUNT?

With all of the previously stated caveats, it's clear that an HSA can be a bit of a gamble. If you are in less than perfect health as you near retirement, you might find the HSA you put in place to save for the future is instead being used to pay for your medical care right now. However, if you are in excellent health (and anticipate that you will remain so), switching to an HDHP plan with an HSA can be a savvy move, particularly if you are concerned about taxes. Since you are contributing pre-tax income to your HSA, you can reduce your tax burden during these all-important years before retirement.

If you have any reason to believe you might deplete your HSA savings before you reach your retirement age, it makes more sense for you to remain on your employer's insurance and save money for your future healthcare costs in a different investment vehicle.

Using a Roth IRA for Retirement Healthcare Savings

Another good option for earmarking healthcare savings is to open a Roth IRA account specifically to pay for medical costs in retirement. The Roth IRA allows you to put money that has already been taxed into the account, where it grows and may be withdrawn tax-free. Unlike its traditional IRA counterpart, there is no up-front tax deduction on contributions. However, as long as you hold onto the account for at least five years and are no younger than fifty-nine-and-a-half when you withdraw your funds, there is no penalty for withdrawals, and they can be used for anything—including medical expenses. In addition, if you enjoy perfect health throughout your retirement and find that you do not need to touch the money you have set aside in the Roth IRA you opened for that purpose, there is no minimum distribution, as there is with a traditional IRA.

One final advantage to Roth IRAs is the relatively high contribution limit. The general contribution limit for 2021 is $6,000, while those who are fifty or older may contribute an additional $1,000. (Please note: These limits are an aggregate of what you can contribute to all of your IRAs if you hold more than one. However, the IRA limits are not related to the limits on contributions to either 401(k) plans or HSAs.) This is another investment vehicle that will work best for you if you are in excellent health. That's because you can invest in more growth-oriented (and therefore, aggressive) stocks and mutual funds since you don't anticipate needing to tap your Roth IRA for ten to fifteen years, if not longer.

However, even if you are not in the best of health, or you know that debilitating illnesses like Alzheimer's run in your family, spending the next five years investing in a Roth IRA can still be a great idea, since it will provide you with tax-free money that you can access for any needs (medical or otherwise) as soon as you've reached the five-year/age fifty-nine-and-a-half milestone.

Healthcare Options If You Retire Before Sixty-Five

While the typical retirement age has long been set (somewhat arbitrarily) at sixty-five, many workers either dream of getting a jumpstart on their retirement or find themselves involuntarily retired before reaching the standard age.

If you hope to retire before you reach sixty-five or you know that you may be forced to retire prior to that age, there are several healthcare options available to you to ensure that your medical costs will not bankrupt you. Here's a breakdown of the options available to retirees who are not yet old enough to qualify for Medicare.

EMPLOYER-PROVIDED RETIREE HEALTH BENEFITS

If you are lucky enough to work for a company that offers health benefits to retirees, jump on it. In almost all cases, this will be your least expensive option for healthcare in early retirement, and it has the added bonus of being a familiar plan that you do not have to learn to navigate. Unfortunately, this once-prevalent perk is slowly going extinct.

According to the Kaiser Family Foundation, only 18 percent of large firms (defined as companies employing two hundred or more workers) offered this benefit in 2018. For comparison, in 1988, 66 percent of large firms offered retiree healthcare benefits.

Even if you work for one of the companies that extends healthcare coverage to retirees, you have to remember that you might not be able to count on it throughout your retirement. First of all, many employers who offer retiree healthcare benefits have an end date of your sixty-fifth birthday, meaning that they will only cover you until you are eligible for Medicare. While that does mean you'll always be covered, it may mean you go from the primo insurance plan offered by your employer to the bare-bones coverage offered by Medicare. If you've never had to pay the premiums for your excellent health insurance, you may get sticker shock when you realize what you will have to pay in premiums for a Medicare Advantage Plan to get the level of care you're used to.

Companies have no legal obligation to cover retired employees—even if they have already provided benefits to retirees. Employers may (and do) reserve the right to change the terms of their healthcare plans, which means that your benefits can potentially be cut or eliminated with no warning or recourse.

THE SUMMARY PLAN DESCRIPTION

One of the many pieces of paperwork you've received (and probably ignored) from your company's HR department is the Summary Plan Description, or SPD, for your health insurance. This is a document that outlines the terms of your healthcare plan, and your employer is required to provide you with a copy within ninety days of your enrollment in the plan. Any time your employer makes a change to its healthcare plan or benefits, you will receive a new SPD. For those retirees who receive benefits in retirement, the SPD in place as of the date of retirement is what's known as the controlling document—that is, the particular SPD that governs your benefits and rights while you are retired. If you don't know where your company's most recent SPD is, ask the folks in HR to provide you with a new copy—and hold onto it!

Retirees who do have health insurance benefits should read over the Summary Plan Description (SPD) for their healthcare plan to determine if they could lose their benefits down the road. Unless there is specific language guaranteeing maintenance of benefits in your SPD, you may find yourself years from Medicare eligibility with no health insurance.

Your SPD will tell you if your employer promises benefits at a specified level for a specified duration. If it does not, you may lose your benefits. Even if the language seems clear that your benefits are guaranteed, it is possible that your employer may change plans or benefits, triggering a new SPD—which could become the controlling document over your benefits. According to the US Department of Labor, when this sort of SPD switcheroo has occurred, some courts of law have upheld the original SPD, while others have allowed the employer to make the switch and thereby cut off the retirees on benefits.

The bottom line when it comes to employer-provided health benefits is that you should take advantage of them if offered, but always be aware that you could lose them with very little notice.

COBRA

If your employer does not offer retiree benefits, you could still continue with the same health insurance through the COBRA (Consolidated Omnibus Budget Reconciliation Act) health benefit provisions. This program provides former employees, including retirees, the option of temporarily continuing their health coverage at the same group rates paid by their employer.

This option is only realistic for those who plan to retire within eighteen months of their sixty-fifth birthday—since COBRA benefits have an upper limit of a year and a half. In addition, just because you are getting the group rate on monthly premiums does not mean those premiums are cheap. According to the Kaiser Family Foundation, as of 2020, the average cost of premiums for an employer-sponsored health plan was $7,470 per year for singles and $21,342 for families. In addition, health insurers are allowed to tack on a 2 percent administrative fee for those former employees who elect to take COBRA benefits, which means you may end up paying 102 percent of the premium costs that you and your employer shared during your career. Considering that these numbers do not include deductibles, copayments, coinsurance, or other medical costs, taking the COBRA option can be out of reach for the average early retiree.

Individual Coverage Through the ACA's Health Insurance Marketplace

As of right now, the future of the Affordable Care Act is very much in limbo. The tax penalty for going uninsured has been reversed, and uninsured taxpayers do not have to pay that penalty as of 2020. Without the penalty, it is unclear there will be enough voluntary sign-ups to keep costs low. With politicians of every stripe claiming to have the solution for our healthcare costs, the only certainty about the future of medical care in America is that it will change.

At the time of this writing, however, the Affordable Care Act is still the law of the land, and it still offers the best options for uninsured individuals who have not yet reached age sixty-five. Here's what you need to know about purchasing a policy through HealthCare.gov:

Understanding the ACA's Health Insurance Marketplace

When shopping for individual health insurance through the Health Insurance Marketplace (which is also called the health insurance exchange or HIX), you will have a choice between four different "tiers" of insurance coverage. Each tier has a different actuarial value (that is, the percentage of health costs paid for by the insurer, rather than the patient), which affects the cost of premiums:

- **BRONZE:** The insurer is responsible for 60 percent of medical costs.
- **SILVER:** The insurer is responsible for 70 percent of medical costs.
- **GOLD:** The insurer is responsible for 80 percent of medical costs.
- **PLATINUM:** The insurer is responsible for 90 percent of medical costs.

The lower the actuarial value of the insurance, the lower the premiums will be. However, there will be higher out-of-pocket costs for any healthcare received through a plan that has a low actuarial value. Nevertheless, even the lowest-cost plans in the bronze tier will have to conform to the ten essential health benefits required by the law. According to the website *ObamaCare Facts*, these minimum benefits are:

1. Ambulatory patient services
2. Emergency services
3. Hospitalization
4. Maternity and newborn care
5. Mental health services and addiction treatment
6. Prescription drugs
7. Rehabilitative services and devices
8. Laboratory services
9. Preventive services, wellness services, and chronic disease management
10. Pediatric services, including dental and vision care

Since all plans in the Health Insurance Marketplace will adhere to these minimum benefits and these tier levels, it will be easier for you to compare apples to apples in determining which plan will work best for you.

COST-SHARING ASSISTANCE THROUGH THE ACA

Individuals and families at or below 250 percent of the federal poverty level will also be eligible for cost-sharing assistance at the silver level. Those with more modest incomes will have the actuarial value of coverage increased so that they do not have to pay the full remaining 30 percent of the cost of services that are covered by insurance. Table 8–2 breaks down precisely what kind of cost-sharing assistance you can expect:

TABLE 8-2:

Cost-Sharing Assistance

PERCENTAGE OF FEDERAL POVERTY LINE	INCOME FOR A FAMILY OF 1 IN 2021 DOLLARS	INCOME FOR A FAMILY OF 2 IN 2021 DOLLARS	ACTUARIAL VALUE OF SILVER COVERAGE
100%	$12,760	$17,240	94%
138%	$17,609	$23,792	94%
150%	$19,140	$25,860	94%
200%	$25,520	$34,480	87%
250%	$31,900	$43,100	73%

OUT-OF-POCKET SPENDING LIMITS

The ACA also sets maximum out-of-pocket spending limits for health insurance accessed through the healthcare marketplace. If you do not qualify for cost-sharing, your out-of-pocket maximum for the year can be no more than $8,550 for an individual or $17,100 for a family as of 2021. If you do qualify for cost-sharing, out-of-pocket costs can be no more than $2,850 to $6,800 for an individual or $5,700 to $13,600 for a family in 2021.

OPEN ENROLLMENT PERIOD

To enroll with a health insurance plan through the ACA marketplace, you must sign up during the open enrollment period. This period generally runs from November 1 to December 15 for the following year, and coverage you sign up for during the open enrollment period goes into effect as of January 1.

If you miss the open enrollment period, you may still be able to qualify for special enrollment. Triggering events that qualify you for special enrollment include losing other healthcare coverage, getting married, or having a baby. In addition, if you qualify for Medicaid, you may sign up for it at any time. You do not have to wait for the open enrollment period.

CHAPTER 8 TAKEAWAYS

☑ According to Fidelity, the average sixty-five-year-old couple retiring in 2020 will need $295,000 in today's dollars to cover their medical expenses in retirement. However, this calculation does not take into account the fact that healthcare needs can fluctuate.

☑ Medigap insurance is private insurance that can help cover the costs that Medicare does not. You cannot have a Medicare Advantage Plan (Medicare Part C) and a Medigap plan at the same time.

☑ Disability insurance can help protect your income in the five years before you retire. Your employer may already provide you with some disability insurance, but you might be able to increase your coverage with an additional policy.

☑ Long-term care insurance will pay for the kind of long-term, non-medical personal care that Medicare does not cover. However, the cost of long-term care insurance means it is the ideal solution for only about 20 to 30 percent of retirees.

☑ A health savings account (HSA) is a tax-advantaged investment account associated with a high-deductible health plan. You may put pre-tax money in your HSA, where it grows tax-deferred, and from which you can make tax-free withdrawals for qualified medical expenses.

☑ A Roth IRA can be a good vehicle for healthcare savings, as you can access the money tax-free in retirement, no matter how you spend the money.

☑ If you retire prior to reaching Medicare eligibility, you may be able to stay on your former employer's health insurance plan if you receive retiree health insurance benefits. Otherwise, you may be able to extend your health benefits for up to eighteen months with COBRA.

☑ You can purchase a health insurance plan through the Affordable Care Act Health Insurance Marketplace during open enrollment each year from November 1 through December 15. If you miss open enrollment, you may qualify for special enrollment if you have lost your insurance or gotten married.

What to Do When

YEARS TO RETIREMENT/AGE	WHAT TO DO
Five	If you don't have health insurance, visit HealthCare.gov to start enrolling in an individual healthcare plan through the ACA Health Insurance Exchange.
Five	Discuss with your financial adviser your options for health insurance, disability insurance, and/or long-term care insurance, as well as opening a Health Savings Account and/or a Roth IRA to pay for future healthcare costs.
Five	Visit your HR department to learn the details of any disability benefits offered through your employer.
Five	Visit multiple insurers to check prices and enroll in disability or long-term care coverage.
Four through one	Meet with your financial adviser at least once a year to evaluate your plans for handling healthcare costs in retirement.
Four through one	Max out your contributions to the previous year's HSA or Roth IRA.
One	Meet with your HR department to discuss if and how your healthcare benefits will change; if you can't find your Summary Plan Description (SPD), request another copy.
One	If you are retiring prior to sixty-five, visit HealthCare.gov to enroll in an individual healthcare plan through the ACA Health Insurance Exchange.
Age fifty-nine-and-a-half	If you have held your Roth IRA for at least five years, you may now begin making withdrawals if you need them.
Age sixty-five	If you are planning on purchasing a Medigap policy, do so within six months of reaching age sixty-five and enrolling in Medicare Part B. Miss this window, and you will have to go through medical underwriting to qualify for a Medigap plan.

3

Home, Family, and Other Considerations

CHAPTER 9

Housing in Retirement

Figuring out where to live when you retire is more complex than dreaming of the adorable cottage on the beach you've always wanted—or even calculating the costs of moving to the adorable cottage. This chapter will go over all of the important questions you need to answer in the next five years so that you can make the right choice for yourself and your family.

Unlike most of the other issues in this book, the questions raised in this chapter may require you to discuss options with your children or other family members. Where you live impacts your family, and getting their input can help determine if your expectations and assumptions for your retirement home align with theirs. A worksheet of questions is included at the end of this chapter that will help you discuss various aspects of your retirement housing plans with your family.

Have You Paid Off Your Mortgage?

The first consideration regarding housing in retirement is whether you have paid off the mortgage on your current home. Traditional experts consider retiring with a mortgage to be a cardinal sin. There are several reasons for this:

1. Since your mortgage payment is likely your largest monthly expense, it makes sense to eliminate it before retirement to make your income go further.

2. You increase your tax burden if you need to take IRA or 401(k) withdrawals in order to pay your monthly mortgage.

3. Having your home paid off means that you have another large asset in your portfolio that is yours free and clear.

However, even with these excellent reasons for having your home completely paid off prior to retirement, a number of retirees are entering their post-career life still carrying a mortgage. A study by the Joint Center for Housing Studies of Harvard University found that as of 2016, 46 percent of homeowners between the ages of sixty-five and seventy-nine carried a mortgage, with a median balance of $77,000. In addition, 26 percent of homeowners age eighty and above also carried a mortgage, with a median balance of $43,000.

Retirees have decided to hold onto a mortgage for various reasons. For instance, any homeowner who currently enjoys a low interest rate on his mortgage may feel that his money will go further if he invests it for his retirement rather than sending extra payments toward his 4 percent mortgage.

To be fair, if the choice is between funding his 401(k) and paying off his mortgage, that hypothetical homeowner would be absolutely correct. That's because he could be missing out on the company match by preempting his savings in order to pay off his mortgage—not to mention the higher percentage rate even the most conservative of investors could assume for their retirement portfolio. If you are in a situation where you only have enough cash to fund your 401(k) or pay off your mortgage, you should certainly move paying off your mortgage to the back burner.

All that said, I feel that most retirees should not enter into retirement with a mortgage. Retirement expenses are high enough (as the rest of this book has likely made clear to you), and there is no reason to unnecessarily add to those expenses if you do not have to. So, if you are five years out from retirement and will not be able to pay off your mortgage in that time, what are your options?

1. **ACCELERATE YOUR MORTGAGE PAYMENTS.** If you are within spitting distance of your payoff date, you can start sending half your monthly mortgage payment every two weeks rather than a full payment once a month. This will ensure that you are an entire month ahead every year, which can cut your interest and your term. This will only work for retirees within five years of retirement if they are in the last few years of their mortgage.

2. **START A SECOND INCOME STREAM.** Whether you decide to rent out a spare bedroom, freelance, or start an eBay resale business, you can find a way to generate some more money to go toward your mortgage payoff goal. This option can be a good plan if you are absolutely committed to staying in your current house mortgage-free in retirement.

3. **DOWNSIZE.** The most efficient method for killing a mortgage before you retire is to sell the house and move to something smaller and less expensive. There are very few downsides to this plan, other than the hassle of moving and the emotional loss you might feel in leaving your home. Overall, downsizing can often be an enormous boon to your retirement plans and finances. We'll take a closer look at the benefits of downsizing later in this chapter.

Deciding to Stay Put

There are any number of reasons why you may want to stay in the house you've called home for a long time, from the memories you've created in that house to a garden-variety hatred of moving. Staying in your current home can be a sound retirement decision, but you should consider various financial issues before you allow nostalgia (or inertia) to make your decision for you.

In particular, your financial considerations when deciding to stay put should include not only the cost of your mortgage, property taxes, and homeowner's insurance but also the cost of maintaining your home, replacing worn-out appliances, and the potential costs of health accommodations to your home. Worksheet 9–1 will help calculate how much it will cost you to stay put, whether you have your mortgage paid off or not.

DON'T FORGET THE COST OF HEALTH ACCOMMODATIONS

Another important cost of staying in your home is making accommodations for reduced mobility as you age. Much of this will depend upon your specific needs and how your home is currently set up. *HomeAdvisor* (www.homeadvisor.com), which helps homeowners determine the costs of various home improvements, calculates that the average cost to remodel for disability accommodations is nearly $9,000 and can be as high as $20,000.

WORKSHEET 9-1:
The Yearly Costs of Staying in Your Current Home

EXPENSE	AMOUNT
Mortgage	$
Property Taxes	$
Homeowner's Insurance	$
Home Maintenance*	$
TOTAL	$

*According to mortgage data firm HSH, a good rule of thumb for home maintenance costs is to expect to spend between 1 percent and 2 percent of the value of your home on maintenance expenses each year (www.hsh.com/first-time-homebuyer/cost-of-owning-a-house.html). In addition, we will be talking in detail about budgeting for home maintenance and replacement costs in Chapter 11. For now, using HSH's rule of thumb can give you a basic idea of what to expect from your housing costs in retirement.

THE DOUBLE-EDGED SWORD OF HOME APPRECIATION

Having your home appreciate in value is most certainly a good thing. However, it also has its very unpleasant downside. Since your property taxes are based upon your home's value, many retirees who purchased homes at relatively low prices may find that their now-hot neighborhood is too expensive to live in, even if their mortgage is paid off.

What about a Reverse Mortgage?

If your current home is either paid off or mostly paid off, then you might be tempted by a reverse mortgage, either to help you eke out your retirement income or to help you pay for your housing costs in a high-cost-of-living area that you have called home for a long time. You see these products touted on daytime television (often by Tom Selleck and his glorious mustache), and they can seem like an easy answer to both money and housing problems. However, there can be some big pitfalls.

HOW A REVERSE MORTGAGE WORKS

A reverse mortgage is just what it sounds like. Instead of borrowing money from the bank that you will have to pay off in installments, the bank lets you tap the equity in the home you own, generally either in a lump sum or in installments, while you live there. You owe closing costs at the time you take the reverse mortgage, which we'll discuss in detail later in this section, and you will be accruing interest throughout the life of the reverse mortgage, which will have to be paid back along with the loan balance at the end of the term. (However, that term does not end until you move permanently, sell the house, or pass away.) Those aspects of a reverse mortgage can make it too expensive for many retirees and their families. In order to qualify for a reverse mortgage, you must meet several eligibility requirements:

- You and your spouse must both be over age sixty-two.
- You must own your home or have a significant amount of equity in it if your mortgage is not entirely paid off. (If you still have a mortgage, you must use the proceeds from the reverse mortgage to pay it off.)
- You must live in the home full-time.

The safest choice for a reverse mortgage is through the HUD program called Home Equity Conversion Mortgage (HECM, often pronounced in the industry as "HECK-um"). This program has established the market values of homes throughout the country that HECM will support, and the loans are federally insured. Proprietary reverse mortgages—private loans that are only backed by the institutions that offer them—cannot provide you with the same level of insurance. In addition, HECM loans require potential borrowers to attend third-party financial counseling by a HUD-approved provider, which will help borrowers to understand exactly what the costs and financial implications will be if they choose to take the loan. While some proprietary reverse mortgage providers also require counseling, many do not.

FINDING A HECM HOUSING COUNSELOR

If you are interested in either taking a HECM loan or simply learning more about reverse mortgages from an impartial source (which I highly recommend if you are thinking of taking a proprietary reverse mortgage), visit www.hud.gov/i_want_to/talk_to_a_housing_counselor or call 1-800-569-4287 for a list of counselors who serve your area. You can expect to pay $125 for the counseling service, which can be paid from your loan proceeds. However, you cannot be turned away from counseling if you are unable to afford the fee.

In addition, HECM loans are readily available in every part of the country and require no credit, income, or medical requirements to qualify. However, HECM loans are not necessarily right for every reverse mortgage borrower. Since HUD has established market values of homes, if you own a home with a much higher value than those of its neighbors, you will not be able to cash out the full value of your home through a HECM loan. Additionally, you may be able to find better interest rates and closing costs through proprietary reverse mortgages, so it may make sense to do some shopping around.

HOW MUCH CAN YOU BORROW THROUGH A REVERSE MORTGAGE?

The amount that you are eligible to borrow depends on a number of factors, including your (and your spouse's) age, the appraised value of your home, and current interest rates. The older the youngest borrower is, the more equity you have in your home, and the lower the interest rate, the more cash you can get out of a reverse mortgage. However, as of 2020, there is a limit of $765,600 on reverse mortgage lending, no matter the home's appraised value.

There are a few ways to receive payments from a reverse mortgage:

- As a lump sum. This option has the highest level of interest and fees.
- In monthly installments. You can either choose to receive your payments for a fixed term or for life—which, if you are a co-owner with your spouse, means for the life of both spouses.
- As a line of credit, which can be withdrawn as needed. This option will maximize the amount of money available to you for withdrawal.
- Through some combination of the first three options.

One more advantage of accessing the equity in your home in this way is that your reverse mortgage payments are entirely tax-free and will generally not affect your Social Security or Medicare benefits. (However, if you do qualify for low-income assistance from the government, such as Medicaid, you may find that the money from your reverse mortgage disqualifies you from such benefits.)

REVERSE MORTGAGE COSTS

Before you decide that the pleasant retirees touting reverse mortgages on the daytime commercials have the right idea, you should know about the costs of these loan products, both now and in the future. One of the big upsides to a reverse mortgage is that it is impossible to be upside down in your mortgage. Even if the value of your house goes down, you cannot owe more than the appraised value of your home at the origination of the reverse mortgage. However, the lender does need to protect itself from such home value dips, and it does so through high origination fees and mortgage insurance. If you are interested in a reverse mortgage, you can expect to pay the following:

- An origination fee that is the greater of $2,500 or 2 percent of the first $200,000 of your home's value, plus another 1 percent for amounts above that, with a cap of $6,000 total for the origination fee
- An upfront mortgage insurance premium of 2 percent of the home's value
- An annual mortgage insurance premium of 0.5 percent of the mortgage balance. This amount will go up each year if you are taking installments
- A monthly servicing charge of up to $35, which gets added to your loan balance each month
- Traditional closing costs

In most cases, retirees who are taking on a reverse mortgage would use the proceeds of the loan to pay these costs, meaning they would have no out-of-pocket expenses. However, no out-of-pocket expenses does not mean there are no costs.

It's important to remember all the ways taking on a reverse mortgage could affect you and your family. To start, there are several ways your loan could come due:

- If you sell the house.
- If you and your spouse die.
- If you can no longer consider your home a primary residence. This goes into effect if you find yourself needing long-term nursing home care for more than twelve months. Up to that twelve-month limit, you can still consider your home a primary residence.
- Since you continue to hold the title to your house, you could be considered in default on the loan if you do not pay your property taxes, do not have adequate homeowner's insurance, or you fail to maintain your home, at which point your loan could become due.

This means you or your family could end up in a tough spot if you lose your ability to care for the house or yourself: You will probably have to sell the house in order to pay the loan.

Even if everything goes as planned, and your reverse mortgage pays you and your spouse monthly installments until you both go to the mortgage-free house in the sky, there could be a potential issue for your family. If you hope to leave your home to your children, they will need enough cash on hand to be able to pay off the reverse mortgage at the time of your death. Otherwise, the bank will sell the house. If there is any equity left, it will go to your family, but depending on how long you have held the reverse mortgage, the sale could leave your heirs with absolutely nothing. In addition, if the loan balance is greater than the value of the home, your children would still have to pay off the full amount of the loan in order to retain ownership.

One final cost to consider is the interest rate on your reverse mortgage. While these rates can be either fixed or variable, you are more likely to be offered a product with a variable rate—making the payoff amount even higher when the loan comes due.

SHOULD YOU TAKE A REVERSE MORTGAGE?

A reverse mortgage can be a useful tool for retirees who are hoping to stay in their paid-off home. If you anticipate that you will have a healthy retirement and you would like to tap into the equity in your largest asset, taking on a reverse mortgage can help you to improve your retirement finances. Just be aware that it's not something to count on—and you should plan for your home passing out of your family's hands.

Deciding to Downsize

Downsizing in retirement can have any number of great benefits—and not just financial ones. For instance, by trading out your family home for something smaller, you can expect to pay off (or at least reduce) your mortgage, reduce your property tax burden, save money on utilities, save money and time on maintenance, and purge a great deal of the stuff you've accumulated over the years—which is not only psychologically freeing but also potentially lucrative.

Downsizing when your home has appreciated a great deal has the added bonus of providing you with more cash to put toward your retirement. While there are capital gains taxes on the profit you make from a home sale, they do not kick in until you are making more than $250,000 from the sale as a single filer, or $500,000 for married couples filing jointly. So if you need to beef up your retirement savings in order to ensure a secure retirement, selling your home can be a good decision.

But what are your options for retirement housing, and how do you choose a new place?

FACTOR IN THE COST OF MOVING

According to Worldwide ERC, an association that tracks the costs of workforce mobility, the average cost to ship household goods in 2014 was just under $13,000. While you can certainly save money by doing some or all of the move yourself, by this time in your life it's a great deal less fun to pack boxes into a U-Haul than it was in your twenties (not that it was particularly enjoyable then). When deciding on where to live in retirement, make sure you include the cost of your move in your calculations. The website *Moving Guru* offers a good calculator for determining the cost of a move at www.movingguru.com/movingcostcalculator. The calculator provides you with three cost options: professional movers who pack up your home and move it; self-pack services where professionals only handle the loading, driving, and unloading; and simple truck rentals.

Deciding Whether to Rent or Buy

When deciding to downsize, the next big question to answer is whether your new home should be a rental or a purchase.

If you cash out enough equity from your home sale, you could potentially buy a new, smaller home with cash, meaning you've traded your equity for a new place to live with lower costs and no mortgage. Score! However, except for some areas of the country, most home sales will likely only provide the seller with enough equity to put a sizeable down payment on another house—putting a retiree back in the position of having a mortgage during retirement. Add to that the amount of money that will be eaten up by closing costs, and it's even harder to determine whether having a mortgage payment or a rent payment is worth your while.

Fortunately, the real estate website *Trulia* has created a formula for determining if you are better off financially by renting or buying. *Trulia* calls this the price-to-rent ratio, and it takes into account the total costs (and tax benefits) of home ownership as well as the total costs of renting a similar property. The price-to-rent ratio is calculated by dividing the average list price of homes in an area by the average yearly cost of renting similar homes in that same area, as follows:

Average list price / Average Yearly Rent = Price-to-Rent Ratio

For instance, if the average list price of three-bedroom homes in an area is $250,000, and the average rent is $1,600 per month, or $19,200 per year, then the ratio would be calculated as follows:

$250,000 / $19,200 = ~13

Trulia then rates these ratios in the following way:

- Price-to-rent ratio of 1–15: Much better to buy than rent
- Price-to-rent ratio of 16–20: Generally better to rent than buy
- Price-to-rent ratio of 21 or higher: Much better to rent than buy

This ratio can give you a picture of the cost dynamic in any particular area of the country, no matter how the market is doing nationally.

Of course, the decision to rent or own in retirement is about more than just dollars and cents. You also need to think about lifestyle issues, such as whether you would prefer to live a maintenance-free life or avoid being tied down. Renting also has the added benefit of helping you to preempt any health-related issues that can affect your housing choices. Not only will you be selling your home early, which will be less stressful (and potentially more lucrative) than having to sell when you become ill or incapacitated or require nursing home care, but it will also be easier for you to make health-related housing decisions if you are not tied to a single spot.

RELOCATING IN RETIREMENT

Many retirees dream of moving someplace warm to spend their golden years, or they plan to move closer to children or family who live elsewhere in the country. Unless you are moving specifically to be closer to your grandchildren, it may be difficult to figure out where you want to relocate. AARP offers some great advice on the best places for retirees to live at https://livindexhub.aarp.org. If you decide to relocate, it's often a good idea to rent for a year or two after you first arrive in order to get the lay of the land, even if you do eventually plan to buy a home.

You will need to consider all these issues while thinking about where you should hang your hat in retirement. The questions in the worksheet at the end of this chapter should help encourage discussion between you and your spouse (and family) to help figure out what course of action works best for your retirement.

Retirement Communities

Of course, there are many more options for seniors than just finding a house or an apartment on their own. You can also choose to move into a retirement community. Unlike the "homes" of yesteryear, these communities can provide retirees with maintenance-free living, a large group of peers as neighbors, planned activities or on-site recreation and leisure facilities, some health and/or mobility support, and the added bonus of not having to yell at teenagers to get off your lawn. There are several different types of retirement communities available. Here's what you can expect from each type:

1. **55+ RETIREMENT COMMUNITIES:** These communities are much like any other gated or planned communities, except that they are age-restricted. In general, you will own your home in such a community, which could be anything from a condo to a vacation-style house to an apartment in a high-rise building. Costs vary from community to community, but in addition to your purchase price, plan on paying a monthly fee for maintenance, services, and amenities. That fee could range anywhere from a couple of hundred to several thousand dollars per month.

2. **INDEPENDENT LIVING COMMUNITIES:** These are much like age-restricted retirement communities, except they tend to also offer a large number of activities and amenities, making them more like all-inclusive resorts than a simple neighborhood community. Generally, homes in independent living communities are leased, which can make this a good option for anyone who does not want to be tied down. Often meals, transportation, utilities, light housekeeping, and all maintenance are covered by your monthly fee. However, prices are steep. Holiday Retirement, a franchised independent living community provider, states that it has an average monthly rent/fee of $2,850. However, that is the average across the country for Holiday's fees; those costs can vary even within Holiday's own communities. (See www.holidayseniorliving.com and www.aplaceformom.com.) In addition, some independent living communities charge buy-in fees or also ask you to purchase your home in addition to paying monthly fees.

3. **ASSISTED LIVING FACILITIES:** This option is for retirees with some health issues who do not quite need skilled nursing facility care. Your rent pays for a private room, along with access to activities and amenities, meals (in some facilities), and access to skilled nursing and medical care on-site. Costs can range between $2,000 and $7,000 per month, but the average cost nationally is over $4,000 per month.

4. **CONTINUING CARE RETIREMENT COMMUNITIES (CCRC):** These are the one-stop shop of retirement communities, and they can take care of seniors for the rest of their lives. CCRCs offer residents options of independent living, assisted living, and skilled nursing home care. As your needs change, you can move from living independently in your own apartment, to getting assistance as necessary, to receiving skilled nursing care, without ever leaving your community. CCRCs require a hefty upfront entrance fee—the average initial payment is $329,000, but that can be as high as $1 million—plus monthly charges that range from $1,000 to $5,000. In addition, those monthly charges may go up if you need to transition from independent living housing to assisted living or nursing care.

While many of these prices may seem awfully steep, a retirement community can be a good option for money-savvy retirees. It pays to calculate your savings by living in a community that offers many services and amenities that you will not have to provide for yourself.

WORKSHEET 9-2:
Questions to Discuss Before Deciding Where to Live

Each of these questions can help get you thinking about both the finances and logistics of housing in retirement.

1 What community resources (such as places of worship, community centers, gyms, etc.) and stores do you need nearby in order to feel at home?

2 How far away are you from your nearest family members? What expectations do you have for local family? (This question is particularly important if you are moving to be closer to family.)

3 Who do you know (and can call on) in your community?

4 If you need to stop driving, how will you get around?

5 How easy or difficult will it be for family or friends to come visit?

6 What maintenance tasks will you have to take care of? What will you do if you can no longer manage those tasks?

7 Will you or your spouse be able to stay independently in your home if the other one passes away?

8 Is it important (to you or to them) that your children inherit your house? (This is an important question to discuss, as your kids might care more or less than you assume they do.)

9 Who can/will help you move if you decide to do so?

10 What aspects of your living situation are most important to you?

11 What items in your home are most important to you?

12 If you decide to sell your home, how quickly will you need it to be sold?

13 Do you have reason to believe that your or your spouse's health will deteriorate?

CHAPTER 9 TAKEAWAYS

☑ Paying off your mortgage prior to retirement can help you reduce your post-retirement living expenses, in addition to giving you another large asset that you can draw on if necessary. Either accelerating your mortgage payments or downsizing can help you finish off your mortgage before you retire.

☑ Make sure you calculate the costs of staying in your current home in retirement. In general, you can expect to spend 1 to 2 percent of your home's value on annual maintenance and repair. However, making disability accommodations can cost significantly more than that.

☑ A reverse mortgage can offer you a way to access the equity in your home while you continue to live there. There are a number of costs associated with a reverse mortgage, so it is a good idea to consult with a HECM housing counselor to make sure you understand what a reverse mortgage will mean for your finances.

☑ Do not forget to factor in the cost of moving if you decide to downsize.

☑ If you decide to relocate, you can determine whether renting or buying makes more sense by determining the price-to-rent ratio. Divide the average list price for homes by the average yearly rent.

Ratios of 1–15 indicate that it is better to buy than rent, and ratios of 21 or higher indicate that it is better to rent than buy.

☑ Retirement communities can provide retirees with maintenance-free living, a community, and potentially some health or mobility support.

☑ In addition to financial concerns, make sure you also consider the logistical and community aspects of your housing choices in retirement.

What to Do When

YEARS TO RETIREMENT	WHAT TO DO
Five	If possible, increase mortgage payments to pay off your mortgage by retirement.
Four	Discuss with your financial adviser various retirement housing options.
One	Fill out Worksheet 9–2 and discuss it with your family.

CHAPTER 10

The Family Fortunes

In a perfect world, every adult member of your family would be able to financially support themselves (and any offspring they have), and you would have no bigger family financial concerns than making sure you've put together an equitable will. However, many families financially rely on one or two people—people who would like to retire eventually, thank you very much.

A lot of generic advice will ignore this fact, leaving retirees floundering in the face of difficult questions: How will your retirement affect your family? Will you be able to retire and still provide the same kind of financial support you always have?

Throughout this chapter, we will discuss the ways that your family can affect your finances and your retirement plans—and vice versa.

Prioritizing Your Retirement

For much of your career, retirement has been a sort of amorphous future possibility. Even if you are a diligent saver, it can be much easier to set aside money for a vacation, your child's college education, or even your child's wedding. Every single one of those goals is concrete.

The difficulty most people have in visualizing retirement can lead to other problems, as well. While you're making a good living, it's tough to say no to your kids if they call with a tale of financial woe. Similarly, you might feel obligated to take care of your parents financially, particularly when you have (what feels like) plenty of money. Unfortunately, getting into these financial habits can make it much more difficult for you to take care of yourself. It can lead to the kind of guilty feelings that extended families are renowned for. There is some truth to the adage that taking care of family is like putting on your own oxygen mask first on a depressurized airplane before helping your child. You will best be able to help your dependent family members if you take care of yourself first. The bottom line is that you must put your retirement savings first, ahead of any help you give to your children or other relatives, ahead of any informal money promises you may have made, and even ahead of taking care of elderly parents. This is particularly true as you finish out the last few years of your career.

If the thought of doing this has you squirming in your seat, you're not alone. The intersection of money and family is a charged subject, and one of the many reasons Thanksgiving dinner can be so uncomfortable. You can change these sorts of money habits before they derail your retirement, although it might be awkward. If financially supporting your family has gotten out of control, there are two things you need to do:

SET BOUNDARIES

One reason it is so difficult to say no to family members is because you feel like your loved ones' problems are your problems. However, their problems become yours only if you let them. This can be a relatively easy boundary to set when it comes to telling your child he or she will have to take out loans or work to pay for college or even that you can't pay for a lavish destination wedding. It becomes much more difficult when it's your elderly parents who are struggling.

If you are currently supporting elderly parents or in-laws, it's time to stop personally bankrolling their care. Instead, use their assets until they are exhausted. That will ensure that your parents are eligible for Medicaid, and it will protect your retirement from a similar fate. This may sound heartless, but it is the best option for the entire family.

HAVE THE TOUGH CONVERSATIONS

Many things go unsaid in families. Not only does no one talk about the fact that Great-Uncle Albert picks his nose at the dinner table, but you and your relatives may assume everyone is in agreement about certain expectations. Your kids take for granted that you'll pick up the tab for their master's degree since you paid for the bachelor's. Your parents might think that they'll move in with you for their twilight years. Your grandkids might assume you're going to be gifting them with a car on their sixteenth birthday.

The only way to combat all the unspoken assumptions is to get everything out on the table. At some point, you need to sit down with your children and parents and talk about finances. If you're not springing for a wedding, let them know now. If you have no idea what kind of financial shape your parents are in, it's time to ask. Money may be a taboo subject, but it will be much easier to deal with hurt feelings and resentment if you talk about the issues and make it clear what you can and cannot do for your family.

None of this is going to be comfortable, but it's an important part of protecting your retirement and your own children's financial futures.

Financial Planning with Your Family in Mind

All that said, there is a great deal that you can do in order to make sure your family is financially taken care of even if you are no longer around. While you do need to make sure that you have the money you need to live on in retirement, the way you put together your estate can make a big difference in your family's life later on.

Life Insurance and Retirement

The primary purpose of life insurance is to replace lost income if you were to pass away. You may feel as though retirement marks the point at which you no longer need life insurance, but there are some reasons why you may consider keeping your life insurance as you transition to retirement.

1. Do you have dependents? By the time most people reach retirement, their dependents are grown and taking care of their own financial issues. However, you don't want to forget about how your death

might affect your spouse's finances. If your retirement is being funded by a pension or an annuity (see Chapter 3), then you should consider whether your spouse's income will be enough by itself. In addition, even though your spouse will be eligible for your entire Social Security payment after you have passed away, the entire household benefit that he was receiving may go down. In addition, it's important to think about how dependent adult children will be affected by your death.

2. Using life insurance as an estate planning tool. Another important reason to keep your life insurance up to date in retirement is the fact that life insurance passes directly to the beneficiary, without having to go through probate. Since life insurance benefits are tax-free if the owner of the policy is also the beneficiary, many savvy retirees will have a life insurance policy in place in order to provide their family with much-needed cash to deal with financial obligations after death.

For instance, if you owe money on your home but you would like it to stay in the family, a life insurance policy can provide your family with the necessary capital to be able to purchase the house from the bank. This is particularly important if you are enrolled in a reverse mortgage (see Chapter 9) but want the old homestead to go to your kids. The basic question to ask yourself when deciding whether you need to maintain your life insurance in retirement is whether anyone would suffer financially from your death. If the answer is yes, then it's a good idea to remain insured.

The best strategy to save money on this is to renew an existing policy rather than buy new life insurance after age fifty. So if you have a policy that is going to lapse sometime in the next five years, talk to your financial adviser and/or insurance agent to find out what it will cost to renew and how it will affect your retirement plans.

However, if you live in one of the thirteen states (or the District of Columbia) that levy estate taxes, or in one of the six states that levy inheritance taxes (which tax your heirs, rather than your estate), then using a life insurance policy as a way to help your heirs pay these taxes may also be a savvy estate planning move. The states that levy estate taxes include Connecticut, the District of Columbia, Hawaii, Illinois, Maine,

Maryland, Massachusetts, Minnesota, New York, Oregon, Rhode Island, Vermont, and Washington. The states that levy inheritance taxes include Iowa, Kentucky, Maryland, Nebraska, New Jersey, and Pennsylvania.

LIFE INSURANCE AND ESTATE TAXES

In the past, life insurance policies were commonly used as a way to provide cash to heirs so they could afford to pay estate taxes. However, the 2017 Tax Cuts and Jobs Act increased the estate tax exemption to $11.58 million for an individual, or $23.16 million for a married couple. This exemption will last until the year 2026, when it will return to the 2017 rate of $5 million for singles and $10 million for couples (adjusted for inflation). This means that the majority of my readers will not likely face federal estate taxation.

Estate Planning

The complexities of planning your estate are vast enough to fill a book. (If you would like to read more about it than what is outlined here, I recommend *The Everything® Wills & Estate Planning Book* by Deborah S. Layton.) For our purposes, I am going to provide a brief outline of the main parts of your estate plan so that you can discuss your options with your financial adviser, your lawyer, and your accountant.

Some of the documents you may want to have in place in order to make sure your family is taken care of include a living will, a power of attorney, and various types of trusts. We're going to talk about each of these in turn.

YOUR WILL

This is the center of your estate plan, and it may be something you already have in place. Many people will decide to draw up a will when they get married, have a child, or experience the death of a loved one.

However, even if you do not have a will already in place, now is an excellent time to write one.

PREVENTING INHERITANCE THEFT

Since the first edition of this book, my family and I have gone through a wrenching experience with inheritance theft. Despite being named as an heir in my father's will, the money he intended for me disappeared from his estate. The person serving as executor and trustee did not act with the heirs' best interests in mind, and the upshot was that my father's wishes were not followed.

Though my father was a damn fine financial planner who helped clients with their estate plans throughout his long career, he fell victim to a common estate planning problem: refusing to think about the worst-case scenario. Like so many of us, Dad did not think about how his surviving loved ones might take advantage of ambiguous language or disregard his wishes because he was no longer there to insist. I have come to learn that this is an all-too-common scenario, and most heirs in this position do not have the ability or resources to pursue legal action after their inheritance has been stolen.

This is why everyone who makes a will should ask this question of the attorney or professional drawing up their estate plan: "Based on how my estate plan is currently set up, how could my wishes be thwarted or ignored?" This question is especially important if a single individual will control the money after your passing. If that is the case, a well-written trust document (which we'll discuss later in this chapter) can ensure that your money will go to the heirs you intend. It's best to assume no one in your life will follow your wishes unless they are legally compelled to, and your estate plan should reflect that. Believing that a loved one would never go against your expressed wishes leaves your heirs vulnerable.

It is uncomfortable to think about your loved ones as untrustworthy, which is why so many people draw up wills that can be exploited. But taking the time to think through the worst-case scenario will ensure that you do not leave a legacy of inheritance theft, strife, resentment, and continued heartbreak.

You may make your will as detailed as you like, so that the distribution of your property can follow your exact wishes. You may also change your will any time you like—and it's prudent to review your will every few years to make sure that everything is still up to date. One of the important choices you will have to make is deciding who will act as your executor. An executor is the person who will handle the logistical details of your estate after you have passed away. The typical duties of an executor include:

- Managing your assets until they have been distributed to your heirs.

- Filing your will with the probate court. Probate court is in charge of ensuring that wills comply with all necessary legal requirements. The court will also get in contact with all beneficiaries and heirs named in the will.

- Terminating your accounts and credit cards, as well as notifying banks and government agencies of your death.

- Setting up an estate bank account. This will allow the executor to accept any payments that are owed to you, such as paychecks or stock dividends.

- Paying debts.

- Paying continuing expenses with estate funds. For instance, your executor might need to pay your utility bills or mortgage while the estate is still being settled.

- Paying taxes. The recently deceased owe a final income tax return, covering the time from the beginning of the tax year to the date of death, and it is the executor's job to get that final return filed.

- Supervising the distribution of property. Once the will has gone through probate, it is the executor's job to make sure everything is distributed according to your instructions in the will.

It's important to choose your executor with care. While it is possible to hire an executor to be paid from your estate—for instance, lawyers will often perform executor services—most people will choose a spouse, a friend, or a family member. Your executor does not have to have legal or financial expertise, but they will need to know you well enough to know where to find important documents, and they need to be able to handle the time commitment necessary to carry out their duties. Talk to the person you have chosen to be your executor before you name him or her in your will.

DYING WITHOUT A WILL

It can be easy to put off writing a will for years, since thinking about your own mortality is no one's idea of a rocking good time. However, dying intestate (that is, without a will) can make your heirs' lives much more difficult. Not only will it be up to the state to decide what happens to your property (which means generally your next of kin get everything); your estate will have to pay for the cost of hiring an administrator, which is the intestate version of an executor, leaving less for your heirs.

YOUR LIVING WILL

Another important part of your estate plan is the living will, also known as an advanced medical directive. This will make it clear what your wishes are for medical care if you are too ill or injured to speak for yourself.

In addition to creating your living will, you may also want to assign someone to be your medical power of attorney. This is an advocate you have chosen to speak on your behalf as it relates to your medical care wishes. Assigning a medical power of attorney can help to circumvent any restrictions on your living will, as some states do not allow all such advanced directives to cover all medical procedures.

POWER OF ATTORNEY

In addition to planning ahead for the possibility of being unable to make medical decisions, it's important for retirees to think about who will handle their finances if they become mentally or physically incapacitated. Designating a power of attorney allows you to decide ahead of time who will be making financial decisions on your behalf.

When you designate someone as your power of attorney, it is very important to specify that you are granting durable power of attorney. Without a durable power of attorney, if you are deemed to be legally incompetent, then your designee can no longer act on your behalf. Including specific language that states the power of attorney either remains in effect or comes into effect after you have been declared incompetent will allow your power of attorney to continue to make decisions on your behalf until your death.

TRUSTS

A trust is a financial vehicle whereby a third party (known as the trustee) holds property placed in trust by the grantor for a beneficiary. The trustee has a fiduciary duty to responsibly handle and invest the money in the trust, so it can be an excellent way to make sure money is available for beneficiaries who might not be able to handle the money on their own. There are any number of other reasons why you might want to set up a trust:

- **COMPLETE CONTROL OVER YOUR ASSETS.** With a trust in place, you can specify exactly when and how your assets will be distributed among your beneficiaries. This is especially helpful for retirees who have children from multiple marriages, since it ensures that the money you intend to go to your children will go straight to them at the time you specify.

- **PROTECTION OF YOUR LEGACY.** If you are concerned about your heirs' spendthrift ways or high debt, a trust can protect the money you intend for them from being seized by their creditors or wasted away through poor money management. You can set up a specific chronology that dictates how much money your heirs will receive at various points in their lives.

- **AVOIDANCE OF PROBATE.** While probate is an important part of executing a will, it's not without drawbacks. First, it takes quite a bit of time to complete the probate process. In addition, probate procedures are all public record, meaning anyone can learn more about your estate than you might want them to know. Finally, probate costs can be expensive, averaging anywhere from 6 to 10 percent of the value of the estate. Setting up a trust allows the assets in trust to pass outside of probate.

- **REDUCTION OF TAXES.** Creating a trust can also help families avoid both gift and estate taxes. There are several basic types of trust that you may decide to use to distribute your property:

  - ○ **TESTAMENTARY TRUST.** This type of trust is outlined in your will and is not created until after you have passed away. The downside to testamentary trusts is that the assets you use to fund it are subject to probate and transfer taxes.

  - ○ **LIVING TRUSTS.** This trust is effective as soon as you open it (which is why it's called "living"), and you can be both the trustee and the grantor. You can choose to make your living trust either revocable—meaning you can change or eliminate the trust altogether at any time—or irrevocable—which means there can be no changes to the trust during your lifetime.

  - ○ **MARITAL OR "A" TRUST.** This kind of vehicle is designed to provide benefits to your surviving spouse while avoiding estate taxes. However, the assets in this sort of trust will be included in the surviving spouse's taxable estate.

  - ○ **BYPASS OR "B" TRUST.** This is also often called a credit shelter trust. For those retirees with a sizeable estate, a bypass trust can offer you the option of sheltering the money in the trust from estate taxes while still providing your spouse with money to live on. The money in the trust will also bypass the surviving spouse's estate, thereby protecting your joint heirs from estate taxes after you are both gone.

  - ○ **GENERATION-SKIPPING TRUST.** This kind of trust will allow you to give assets to your grandchildren or great-grandchildren without it having to go to your children first. That can help protect the assets from both potential mismanagement and your children's estate taxes.

  - ○ **IRREVOCABLE LIFE INSURANCE TRUST.** This allows you to remove life insurance proceeds from your taxable estate.

○ **QUALIFIED PERSONAL RESIDENCE TRUST.** This removes the value of your home from your taxable estate.

○ **QUALIFIED TERMINABLE INTEREST PROPERTY (QTIP) TRUST.** This kind of trust is common in blended families, as it provides a surviving spouse with income during his or her life, but the assets will go to additional beneficiaries after the death of the surviving spouse.

○ **SPECIAL NEEDS TRUST.** If you have a dependent or family member with special needs, this kind of trust will financially provide for your loved one without compromising his or her ability to qualify for Medicaid, Social Security insurance, or any other disability-based government benefits.

Trusts can help you to solve otherwise difficult estate planning dilemmas, but they are not necessarily for everyone. Depending on the complexity of your trust, it can cost up to several thousand dollars for your attorney to draw it up. In addition, if your estate is relatively simple and you do not have any particular concerns about how to distribute your assets to your heirs, a trust may be unnecessary. However, it is always prudent to ask yourself how your estate could be stolen, misdirected, or frittered away without a trust in place. Trusts are not foolproof, nor are they always necessary, but it is worthwhile to think through how your estate will get to your heirs. A little forethought now can help you make sure your wishes are carried out.

As with every complex financial decision you make, be sure to discuss all of your estate planning options with your financial adviser. He or she can help you determine the best way to create an estate plan that satisfies your wishes and protects your family.

CHAPTER 10 TAKEAWAYS

☑ Prioritize your retirement savings ahead of helping your elderly parents, adult children, or other family members. Drawing this boundary can be difficult, but it will spare your loved ones further financial headaches in the future.

☑ Retirees may also want to keep a life insurance policy in place after ending their career. Not only can it ease your family's financial stress after losing any retirement income that is yours alone, but life insurance can also be an estate planning tool, since life insurance benefits are not subject to probate or estate taxes.

☑ Your will is the center of your estate plan, and everyone needs one. Dying intestate means the state decides what happens to your assets.

☑ The best way to ensure that your wishes are carried out is to write your will and estate plan to be as legally airtight as possible. Do not assume that your loved ones will follow your wishes; ensure that they will because your estate plan documents give them no choice.

☑ Appointing an executor is one of the most important decisions you will make when drawing up your will. The executor is charged with handling the logistical details of your estate after you have passed away, such as distributing your assets to your heirs, terminating your accounts, and filing your final tax return.

☑ A living will spells out your wishes for medical care if you are too ill or injured to speak for yourself.

☑ Power of attorney designates who will be making financial decisions on your behalf if you are not mentally or physically capable of making decisions for yourself.

☑ A trust allows you to transfer assets to your heirs or beneficiaries based upon rules and conditions that you set. Trusts can offer you a way to ensure that your wishes are carried out.

What to Do When

YEARS TO RETIREMENT	WHAT TO DO
Five	Discuss estate planning with your financial adviser.
Five	Revisit your will, or, if you've not written one, consult an attorney and have one drawn up.
Five	Designate a durable power of attorney.

CHAPTER 11

Creating a Budget on a Retirement Income

Learning how to live on a fixed income can be quite a tough transition if you're used to a steady paycheck. This chapter will teach you how to prepare for both the expected and unexpected changes to your budget that come after you retire. The good news is that you'll save some money by not working, which can help you balance your post-retirement budget. You'll also learn how to plan ahead for everything from your daily activities to replacing your durable goods. By the end of this chapter, you'll feel confident about your retirement budget.

Budgeting after you retire is a different beast from budgeting during your career. While budgeting skills and basics will always remain the same, there are some specific aspects of retirement budgeting that you will need to plan for in order to ensure your comfortable retirement. For instance:

1. Budgeting on a fixed income gives you less wiggle room than budgeting while you could expect regular raises or bonuses or you could take overtime for extra income.

2. As we discussed in Chapter 8, healthcare in retirement can put a bigger dent in your budget than you are used to, even if you are enrolled in Medicare and start your retirement in excellent health.

3. Inflation is a consistent concern in retirement. While inflation certainly affects everyone, you were likely more able to take it in stride while you were working.

4. As Chapter 6 explained in detail, taxes can become more difficult to figure out and file when you are no longer working for an employer.

5. Many of the activities that you have dreamed about enjoying in retirement may end up costing more than you anticipate.

6. One-time big expenses, such as a new car or a roof replacement on your home, can already be difficult to budget for when you are working. If you do not plan for them in retirement, those kinds of expenses can seriously derail your budget.

We have talked in detail about several of these expenses, and we have already calculated how much you will need to budget for several of these unique-to-retirement expenses. However, there are still several retirement costs that can overwhelm a retiree who has not planned ahead for them. These include the cost of retirement activities, the cost of replacing durable goods, and, happily, the amount of money you can expect to save by no longer working.

Even though you will have to do some more homework to determine your yearly expenses, there is some good news. By the time you reach retirement, budgeting may be different, but it should also become easier. For instance, after living in your home for many years, you know that your water heater has a ten-year lifespan, so having to replace it after a decade should no longer be a shock. When you first moved into the house, you might not have had any idea what to expect from your appliances and other durable goods.

However, in order to manage those expectations, you need to know what they are. That may include calculating things like finances, expenses, and the lifespans of your various goods, but it starts with something more fun: sitting down with your spouse and figuring out what you want from retirement. If you have not yet thought about what your retirement will look like—whether you plan to spend your days babysitting your grandchildren, working in the garage, traveling to destinations you never thought you'd see, or just sitting on the sofa in your sweatpants—it's high time that you do.

WORKSHEET 11-1:

What Will My Retirement Look Like?

Think about all the different things you hope to do in retirement. Do you want to spend more time on your hobbies? Do you want to spend less time cooking or cleaning or taking care of your home? Do you want to travel? How often?

Take some time to think about how you will spend your days, weeks, months, and years to determine your retirement hopes and expectations. Writing down these ideas will not only help you to plan financially; it will also give you an opportunity to figure out how your life will change and how it will stay the same post-retirement.

1. Describe a typical day post-retirement.

   YOU: ....

   ....

   YOUR SPOUSE: ....

   ....

2. Describe a typical week post-retirement.

   YOU: ....

   ....

   YOUR SPOUSE: ....

   ....

3. Describe a typical month post-retirement.

   YOU: ....

   ....

   YOUR SPOUSE: ....

   ....

4. Describe a typical year post-retirement.

   YOU: ....

   ....

   YOUR SPOUSE: ....

   ....

Now that you have a better sense of what you and your spouse hope to do in retirement, you can start to plan for your retirement budget.

Depending on what you hope to do with your time, you can expect to either reduce or expand your financial needs. Now is the time to get a clearer picture of exactly how much money you can expect to spend during a typical year of retirement. While we have already come up with rough numbers for this in Chapter 1 (on Worksheet 1–1), you'll have a much clearer idea of your financial needs after you have calculated how retirement will change your expenses in Worksheets 11–2 and 11–3.

WORKSHEET 11-2:
Anticipated Retirement Savings

To calculate your savings regarding car costs, you will have to do a little math prior to filling in the following table. If you can sell your car, then you will need to calculate your monthly savings on your car payment, insurance, gasoline, and maintenance; add them together; and multiply by 12 in order to find your yearly savings:

Car Savings When Selling a Car at Retirement

Car Payment + Insurance + Gasoline + Maintenance* × 12 = Yearly Savings

.... + ... + ... × 12 = ...

*Refer to the maintenance costs you calculated in Worksheet 2–2 in Chapter 2 to estimate this amount.

If you plan on keeping your car, however, you can still potentially save money on your car expenses after you retire. For this calculation, figure out how many miles you drive per day for work. Include any driving you do to get to and from lunch in your mileage calculation. Then multiply that number by 250, which is the typical number of days a full-time employee works per year (at five days per week for fifty weeks out of the year). Once you have your yearly work-related mileage, multiply the mileage by $0.56 (the IRS deductible mileage expense for 2021 and generally accepted as the amount it costs to drive per mile).

Car Savings When No Longer Driving to Work

Miles per Day × 250 = Miles Per Year × $0.56 = Yearly Savings

.... × 250 = ... × $0.56 = ...

Now you're ready to calculate how much you'll save by not working:

Anticipated Savings from Retirement

EXPENSE	HOW MUCH YOU CURRENTLY SPEND PER MONTH BECAUSE YOU WORK	MULTIPLY BY	ANNUAL SAVINGS
Car	$	× 12	$
Clothing	$	× 12	$
Dining out	$	× 12	$
Dry cleaning	$	× 12	$
Tolls/parking	$	× 12	$
Public transportation	$	× 12	$
Personal care	$	× 12	$
Convenience purchases*	$	× 12	$
Professional services†	$	× 12	$
Stress relief**	$	× 12	$
Professional subscriptions or tools	$	× 12	$
Conference costs	$	× 12	$
Other expenditures	$	× 12	$
TOTAL	$		$

*Convenience purchases include everything from the convenience foods you purchase because you have little time for cooking while working, to the purchases you make without shopping around because of time constraints. This can be a tough calculation and is often easiest to figure out in terms of convenience food purchases if you know that you will be cooking more in retirement. If you do not have a good sense of how much you and your spouse spend on convenience, feel free to skip this line item—and be pleasantly surprised when your additional time spent on purchases saves you money.

†Professional services can include house cleaners, lawn care, painters, professional drivers/airport shuttles (if you travel a great deal for work, for example), and other services that you will take care of yourself in retirement.

**Stress relief can include things like massages, spa treatments, chiropractors, and other self-care that you use in order to relieve the stress of working.

Of course, we're not quite done yet. In addition to the money you save by no longer working, you might be spending more money on travel and hobbies. This is where you might use some of those post-career savings. In order to calculate how much your preferred retirement activities will cost, use Worksheet 11–3: Anticipated Retirement-Related Expenses.

WORKSHEET 11–3:
Anticipated Retirement-Related Expenses

EXPENSE	AMOUNT	MULTIPLY BY	ANNUAL AMOUNT
Hobbies	$	× 12	$
Memberships (including country clubs)	$	× 12	$
Local travel	$	× 12	$
Mortgage for vacation home	$	× 12	$
Holiday/family travel*	$	× 4	$
Vacation travel	$	× 1	$
TOTAL	$		$

*If you do not live in the same state as your family—particularly your grandchildren—you may need to calculate for more than quarterly visits. If, however, you would only travel to see extended family once a year (for Thanksgiving, for example), you could calculate for yearly visits instead.

At this point, it's a good idea to determine if your anticipated savings and expenses have left you in the black—or in the red. Again, this is just a simple question of subtraction.

WORKSHEET 11–4:
Spending More or Spending Less in Retirement?

Retirement Savings	$
Retirement Expenses	– $
BALANCE	$

If you find that your retirement expenses will be higher than the savings you will see from no longer working, there is no need to feel discouraged. You can either scale back some of your planned activities or start now to build up more of a cushion in your retirement nest egg for fun money. Since you are taking the time to calculate these expenses while you still have several years to go before you retire, you have the time to devote to enlarging your nest egg. This is one of the smartest things you can do while preparing for retirement, according to Gary Foreman, editor and founder of *The Dollar Stretcher* (www .thedollarstretcher.com). He advises, "It's always a good idea to think about what the future will bring before you hit a major milestone— whether that milestone is becoming a parent or becoming a retiree."

While planning for your fun retirement expenses is probably one of the most enjoyable parts of post-retirement budgeting, this is not quite the end of your calculations. In addition to the potential fun expenses you will face in retirement, you cannot forget about the regular one-time expenses for which you'll have to budget. You'll still have to maintain and replace your durable goods—even though you might have a better sense of the lifespan of those goods once you hit retirement. Before we create the definitive yearly retirement budget, we need to take a look at those large one-time expenses and budget for them. You will use Worksheet 11–5, adapted from Henry K. "Bud" Hebeler's Replacement Budgeting worksheet on his website *Analyze Now!* (www.analyzenow.com).

WORKSHEET 11–5:

Budgeting for Replacement Expenses

ITEM	COST TO REPLACE	LIFE IN YEARS (Estimated)	CURRENT AGE	COST/YEAR (Cost to Replace/Estimated Life)	UNITS TO BUY (30 Years of Retirement + Current Age of Item/Estimated Life)	TOTAL AMOUNT TO SAVE (Cost to Replace × Units to Buy)
Car 1	$	8		$		$
Car 2	$	8		$		$

ITEM	COST TO REPLACE	LIFE IN YEARS (Estimated)	CURRENT AGE	COST/YEAR (Cost to Replace/Estimated Life)	UNITS TO BUY (30 Years of Retirement + Current Age of Item/Estimated Life)	TOTAL AMOUNT TO SAVE (Cost to Replace × Units to Buy)
Replace roof	$	25		$		$
Exterior paint	$	10		$		$
Large-screen TV	$	7		$		$
Furnace	$	20		$		$
Carpet	$	15		$		$
Air-conditioning	$	10		$		$
Interior paint	$	5		$		$
Drapes	$	15		$		$
Computer	$	5		$		$
Freezer	$	20		$		$
Hot water heater	$	10		$		$
Dishwasher	$	15		$		$
Refrigerator	$	20		$		$
Washing machine	$	15		$		$
Dryer	$	15		$		$
Mattress	$	10		$		$
Exercise equipment	$	15		$		$
TOTAL	$			$		$
				(Yearly Total)		*(Retirement Total)*

The yearly total is the amount you will need to have set aside from your yearly budget to be prepared for these replacement costs. The retirement total is the amount you will need to have set aside within your nest egg in order to cover all the replacement costs you will see throughout your retirement.

If the number you came up with for your overall retirement replacement budget seems high, there is no need to panic. First, using non-whole-number units skews the total amount needed to a higher amount. Secondly, your yearly replacement budget total is likely more doable. Plan on putting that amount of your yearly retirement income into either a high-yield savings account or a CD for use when you need to make replacements. Doing that on a monthly (or yearly) basis will ensure that you have the liquid cash you need to handle replacement costs without taking an enormous bite out of your income for any particular year. Finally, many of the durable goods that you will have to replace can be made to last longer or cost less with regular mainte-nance and a willingness to do some tasks—such as interior painting—yourself. So if you are concerned about the amount of your retirement income that will be eaten up by replacing items, start looking for ways to help your goods, appliances, and home necessities last longer.

CHAPTER 11 TAKEAWAYS

☑ To create your post-retirement budget, start by imagining how you would like your ideal day, week, month, and year to look in retirement.

☑ Ending your career can also mean saving money. Calculate how much money you will no longer need to spend on job-related expenses, such as transportation and a work wardrobe.

☑ Calculate how much your anticipated retirement activities will cost to see if your budget balances. If not, tweaking your plans now can help you get your budget in the black.

☑ Make sure you plan ahead for your eventual need to replace durable goods in retirement. Making this kind of replacement a line item in your budget will mean you are not caught flat-footed when your home needs a new roof.

What to Do When

YEARS TO RETIREMENT	WHAT TO DO
Three	Consult with your financial adviser on your post-retirement expenses and income.
One	Draw up a tentative retirement budget.
At retirement	Refine your retirement budget, revisiting every six to eight months to make adjustments as needed.

CHAPTER 12

Common Retirement Pitfalls

WHAT YOU'LL LEARN IN THIS CHAPTER

There are a number of common pitfalls that can derail a retirement plan. In this chapter, we'll discuss the ten most common ways that pre-retirees and retirees can stumble in the path to retirement, including the common scams you might face as you transition to retirement. Just because many retirees fall victim to these common mistakes doesn't mean that you will. Everyone may make mistakes, but having the necessary foreknowledge to avoid these pitfalls can keep you from jeopardizing the retirement you want and deserve. You'll learn what to do and what not to do to ensure that your retirement is secure.

When I was a child, I struggled with perfectionist tendencies and would get very angry with myself whenever I made a mistake. My mother used to reassure me by saying, "Everyone makes mistakes. That's why they put erasers on pencils."

The unfortunate truth, though, is that some mistakes are much costlier than others, and we don't always get a do-over if we've screwed up. This can definitely be the case with making financial mistakes in planning your retirement—not to mention making mistakes once you've taken the retirement plunge. With limited time to recover from mistakes and the high consequences you face if you make one, it's clearly better to avoid these retirement planning mistakes than try to recover from them.

Retirement Pitfall #1:
Relying on Factors Outside of Your Control

While you might roll your eyes at someone who talks dreamily of the day his ship will come in and what he'll do with all that imaginary wealth, near-retirees will often make the exact same mistake. They will make their plans for retirement contingent on things they cannot control.

For instance, debt-payoff expert Dave Ramsey has suggested that the average investor can count on a 12 percent return on his or her investments. While I have a great deal of respect for Mr. Ramsey's advice on becoming debt-free, his suggestion that anyone can expect 12 percent investment returns is simply irresponsible. Ignoring where Ramsey got his particular numbers (since market returns are historically closer to 10 percent), all investors need to take to heart the fact that past returns are no guarantee of future results. (Everyone should have that piece of financial wisdom embroidered on a pillow, or even tattooed on an arm.) Counting on a particular return to have the retirement you dream of means you've given up control over your own future. You cannot control the market—although you have complete control over how much you save and how much you spend.

Similarly, expecting to inherit money from a wealthy relative is foolhardy as a retirement scheme. Not only do wealthy relatives have the disconcerting habit of living what seems like forever, but they also sometimes fall for beautiful young things or idealistic causes in their final years, meaning they change their wills.

Every individual who plans to retire needs to recognize that he or she can only count on his or her own actions. Markets are volatile, promises can be reneged, and nothing is guaranteed. But you have complete control over your money and your plans, and you can change both as needed.

Retirement Pitfall #2:
Overreacting to Market Volatility

As I write this update in mid-November 2020, the market has been on a long, strange trip in reaction to COVID-19 and its attendant changes to our society. While the frightening and sudden market downturns of February and March of 2020 have rebounded, the roller coaster ride of market volatility in 2020 has often been scarier than anything in a Jordan Peele horror film. People may be wondering if the most prudent course of action would be to cash out their portfolio and bury the money in the backyard, especially if they're only just now getting comfortable being in the market again after the 2008 market crash.

Feeling the urge to take the money and run is a perfectly natural reaction to a sudden market downturn. When we see our investments take a huge hit basically overnight, it's difficult to stop our inner Chicken Littles from freaking out over the sky falling.

But jumping at every downturn is the way both madness and lost revenue lie. The market tends to return around 10 percent over time. That means investors need to weather downturns and trust that the market will recover. Otherwise, getting out of the game after a loss means that you have made a temporary loss a permanent one.

According to Joni Clark, president and chief executive officer of 320 Park Analytics LLC, "everyone who converted to cash in 2008—especially after the market dropped—locked in those losses, which meant they also missed the market surges that took place in 2009. Investors who sold out of the equity market for the safety of cash in early March may have locked in losses of close to 25 percent for the year-to-date 2009, and may have missed out on a 58 percent stock market rebound (as measured by the S&P 500 Index)."

Our tendency to overreact to losses in this way is a symptom of the cognitive bias called loss aversion. This weird quirk of our brains makes us work harder to avoid a loss than to earn a gain. For whatever reason, our brains are wired to make us feel losses more keenly than we enjoy gains. Paying daily, weekly, or monthly attention to your portfolio can tempt you to get out of investments that are only taking a temporary dip. It's far more productive to look at your investments no more often than quarterly. By limiting your exposure to the information, and with the help of your financial adviser, you can make more rational decisions.

The other side of the market overreaction coin is continuing to sit on investments that are going gangbusters in the hopes that they will keep going up and up. While it is always possible to liquidate investments before they reach their peak, the greater likelihood is that waiting will only result in losses. It doesn't feel particularly good to kick yourself after either of those scenarios—but wouldn't it hurt more to lose money because you sat on an investment until the price started falling?

Retirement Pitfall #3: Inactivity

After reading through the last pitfall, you may be thinking that the best thing to do when managing your investments is absolutely nothing. That will keep you from meddling with investments when they need time to grow.

While this is an excellent goal, having a set-it-and-forget-it mindset about your retirement investment vehicles also means you will miss out on growth. If you never review your investment strategy or regularly rebalance your portfolio, you could find yourself looking back on years of lost opportunities.

The best way to maximize your investment opportunities is to diversify your assets and meet regularly with your financial adviser to rebalance your portfolio. Joni Clark's advice is specific on this point: "Define your plan for diversifying, and then rebalance regularly, whether once a quarter, once every six months, or once a year. Sell the assets with the most growth to bring your portfolio back into alignment with your plan, and use that to meet your withdrawal requirements. This approach forces you to sell high, something everyone tries to do, but few actually accomplish."

This approach is not only crucial in the lead-up to retirement; it is also a necessary part of your post-retirement strategy. Being proactive and making savvy asset choices can ensure that your nest egg lasts for the long haul.

Retirement Pitfall #4: Retiring Without Your First Three Years' Income Set Aside

One of the distressing aspects of the 2008 market downturn was watching those who had planned to retire that year lose a huge portion of their nest egg just as they were ending their career. Those retirees found themselves in the unenviable position of either having to continue working past their target retirement date or having to figure out a way to cut their living expenses in order to stretch their reduced nest egg.

There is no way to predict the future, so it is entirely possible that anyone reading this book may find himself in a similar situation. However, rather than simply accept that your long-term investments might have to be sold at a terrible time, you can protect yourself by making sure you have created an early retirement bucket. (See Chapter 3 for a full explanation of the bucket method for retirement.)

In short, rather than have all of your savings tied up in long-term investments up until the day you say sayonara to the office, you should have the equivalent of one to three years' worth of living expenses set aside in short-term and conservative assets, such as short-term bonds, money market funds, and cash equivalents. If you retire at the bottom of a market downturn, you have built in enough of a cushion to allow your long-term assets to recover without having to sell them at a time that will cripple your nest egg for the rest of your retirement.

Talk to your financial adviser now about creating such a short-term bucket, since you will want to start transferring assets there within the next couple of years in order to be prepared for your first few years of retirement.

Retirement Pitfall #5:
Taking a Loan from Your 401(k)

This is an enormous no-no at any time in your career, but it's a particularly disastrous mistake if you're within five years of your retirement. Money removed from your 401(k) is money that cannot grow (with compound interest!), even if you are able to pay it back relatively quickly. The lost time equals lost growth, which you cannot afford to waste. In addition, 401(k) loans are considered withdrawals—with the attendant 10 percent early-withdrawal penalty plus income taxes—if you lose or leave your job before paying it back. Add the fact that most 401(k) plans will not allow you to contribute money to the plan while you have an outstanding loan, and it's clear that this kind of loan is going to be extremely costly for you.

If you need a loan, it's far better to explore taking a home equity loan or borrowing from your insufferable brother than taking money from your own future. Yes, the interest on 401(k) loans tends to be low, and you are paying that interest to yourself. But the potential costs and risks are far too high, especially for those who are in their final years of work.

Retirement Pitfall #6:
Taking Money from Your Retirement Plan Prior to Age Fifty-Nine-and-a-Half

Whether you are planning to retire in your fifties, or you feel as if you need to cash out your 401(k) or IRA before hitting the minimum age requirement, you're going to have to wave goodbye to a major chunk of your money. As we discussed in Chapter 6, the rules for early distributions of tax-deferred accounts are very clear: If you take your money early, then you owe Uncle Sam 10 percent of your withdrawal plus regular income taxes. The only exceptions to this are if you take a distribution for a qualified first-time home purchase or because you have become disabled.

No matter how early you hope to retire, it's better to think of your retirement accounts as being completely off-limits until you hit retirement age.

THE LAST RESORT EXCEPTION TO THE FIFTY-NINE-AND-A-HALF WITHDRAWAL RULE

Though the minimum age requirement is an important deterrent to keep you from accessing your retirement funds prior to age fifty-nine-and-a-half, there is an important exception, known as IRS rule 72(t). Under this rule, you may withdraw money penalty-free from your 401(k) or 403(b) prior to age fifty-nine-and-a-half. Under this rule, you may take at least five yearly substantially equal periodic payments (SEPPs), the amount of which is determined by your life expectancy, using an IRS-approved calculation.

Using rule 72(t) to access your money early should be a last resort, however. Whatever money you take from your 401(k) or 403(b) may not cost you a 10 percent early-withdrawal penalty, but it is still money that is missing from your account. That means it is not growing and will affect your future financial stability. There is a very good reason why the IRS makes this a difficult hoop to jump through: They want you to keep your money where it will do you the most good in your retirement.

Retirement Pitfall #7:
Forgetting to Account for Healthcare Costs

As we discussed at length in Chapter 8, healthcare can be an enormous expense in retirement. With the current estimates at $295,000 for healthcare costs in retirement for a sixty-five-year-old couple retiring in 2020, forgetting to factor in the cost of staying healthy can really send your retirement off the rails.

Make sure you have a plan in place to handle the inevitable costs of healthcare. Refer back to Chapter 8 for specific ideas on how to do this.

Retirement Pitfall #8:
Carrying Debt Into Retirement

According to a 2020 analysis by the Employee Benefit Research Institute (EBRI), based on data collected from the Federal Reserve's 2019 Survey of Consumer Finances, 68.4 percent of American families headed by an adult aged fifty-five or older are carrying debt. On average, these indebted 55+ households owed over $82,000.

The study does clarify that mortgage debt makes up the majority of the money that Americans over fifty-five owe. While a mortgage is generally more manageable than other types of debt, the numbers as a whole are still disturbing. Entering your retirement with debt hanging over your head means you are limiting how far your retirement income can go. And did you really save all these years just to send a big chunk of your retirement income to creditors?

While it's a good idea to pay off your debt prior to retirement, that is not always possible. The other option is to reevaluate your expectations for your living standard now and in retirement, so that you do not have to be in debt to maintain an unsustainable lifestyle.

We will talk in detail about adjusting your lifestyle expectations in Chapter 13. For now, suffice it to say that out-of-control debt is like financial cancer: It has the potential to grow and destroy everything you've worked for.

If you are carrying significant debt, now is the time to start digging yourself out of it. Prioritize your payment strategy to destroy high-interest debt, such as credit card debt and car loans, first. If you feel as if you have to choose between paying down debt and saving for retirement in the next five years, then it's time to look for places to cut expenses so that you can do both. As we mentioned in Chapter 2, your first priority is to save up to the employer-matching amount in your 401(k), and after that you should focus on eliminating consumer debt.

If dealing with your debt is an overwhelming prospect, consider working with a credit counseling service. Please note, these are not the same as debt settlement services. Debt settlement programs will often advise clients to stop paying their bills and instead send their money to the settlement program, which will work to persuade the creditors to settle for a smaller amount. However, not all creditors are willing to accept such terms, and clients enrolled in settlement programs sometimes have to declare bankruptcy.

Nonprofit credit counseling agencies, on the other hand, will help consumers create a spending plan based upon their budget, as well as help them create a debt management plan in conjunction with their creditors to help reduce fees and penalties. You can find a credit counseling agency near you at www.nfcc.org.

Retirement Pitfall #9: Taking Social Security Too Early

In Chapter 5, we talked at length about the enormous difference you will see in your benefits if you time your Social Security just right. A too-early enrollment can cost you up to 30 percent of your benefits. Just because you can start receiving Social Security benefits at age sixty-two does not mean that you should. This is an issue that many retirees get wrong. Take the time to figure out your optimal Social Security enrollment schedule now, so that you can plan your other retirement income sources around it. For more information on how to figure out the best time frame for Social Security benefits, refer back to Chapter 5.

Retirement Pitfall #10: Scams

Scamming retirees is a big business. According to the Securities and Exchange Commission (SEC), in 2016, experts estimated that seniors (age sixty and over) in the state of New York lose $352 million to $1.5 billion per year to financial exploitation. There are no current national estimates for the amount of money retirees lose to financial exploitation each year, but considering the estimates just for the state of New York, it's safe to assume the number is massive.

It's easy to see why retirees and the elderly are such tempting targets for scammers and con artists. Not only are retirees sitting on large nest eggs that they might not feel confident handling, but after years of being the head of the household and financial decision-maker for the family they are also likely to be uncomfortable asking children or family members for advice.

Scammers will take advantage of such discomfort by being "sincere" and "trustworthy." As we discussed in Chapter 4, it's an excellent idea to cultivate a sense of paranoia when it comes to anyone who seeks you out to offer a solution to a problem. It is far better for you to be the one searching for someone to help you than to accept the help of someone who sought you out.

That being said, it's also important to remember just how scammers work. Their goal is to either get hold of your money or your identity. Here are the most common ways they will try to do so:

1. **ASKING.** We have gotten used to the Hollywood vision of a hacker—someone who is able to figure out and unlock the security systems of major corporations and government programs through the power of excellent computer skills. However, the majority of hackers and scammers are more like the Melissa McCarthy character in the film *Identity Thief*. In that movie, she manages to steal Jason Bateman's identity by calling him and pretending to be from his bank. He willingly gives her his Social Security number and birth date. No special hacking skills are necessary when many intelligent people don't think to question a call from an official-sounding person. Any time you get a call or email asking for verification of your information, tell them you'll call back (or don't respond to the email). Then, call the institution yourself to see if the contact was legitimate.

2. **PUTTING DOLLAR SIGNS IN YOUR EYES.** Believe it or not, there are still people who fall for the Nigerian email scam—the one where a wealthy Nigerian needs your help transferring his riches to America and is willing to show his appreciation with a big cut of the cash. Though this is one of the crudest of the greed-based scams out there, as a near-retiree you're likely to run into many subtler schemes that promise you the moon in exchange for a small initial investment. Don't let the dollar figure the scammers dangle in front of you make you lose your skepticism. Things that sound too good to be true almost always are.

3. **PEER PRESSURE.** One easy way to make your decision seem like a no-brainer is for the scammer to make it seem as if you'll miss out if you pass up on the opportunity. If someone tells you that many other savvy investors have jumped on this chance, you might find yourself following the herd mentality rather than asking the tough questions yourself.

4. **TIME CONSTRAINTS.** Giving you a very quick deadline for a decision is a tried-and-true sales technique that plays on our fear of losing out on a deal. You'll see it everywhere from one-click ordering on Internet shopping sites to pitches stating that this particular deal on a car/appliance/real estate is only valid for one day. Scammers will often tell you that there is no time to think things over or that a price will go up if you hesitate. But there is no legitimate investment, purchase, or other deal that cannot wait at least twenty-four hours for you to sleep on it and do some independent research.

5. **PLAYING THE EXPERT.** If you feel overwhelmed by financial decisions, it can be a relief to come across someone who clearly knows what she is doing and is willing to make the tough decisions for you. But a con artist doesn't actually have to know her stuff to be able to fake it convincingly. If someone is really trying to sell you on her expertise—either by assuring you that her very important position means she would never recommend something subpar or by dazzling you with finance babble that you simply don't understand—then you need to be very cautious with her advice. Real experts know that they don't know everything, and they don't try to convince you otherwise.

For every single one of these tactics, there is one excellent solution: Ask a lot of questions. Not only will that help you to better understand exactly what is being offered (in the case that it's legitimate), but it also gives you the space to make a rational decision rather than allow your emotions to be manipulated.

In addition, con artists hate dealing with a questioner. It gets in the way of their scam. If you're in a one-on-one situation when you start your Riddler routine, scammers will back away to protect themselves. If you're in a free-lunch seminar or other group setting when you start asking questions, you will likely get the stink-eye or otherwise be silenced so as not to mess up the deal with all of the others. Either way, the response you get to your questions can tell you what you need to know about the legitimacy of the deal.

CHAPTER 12 TAKEAWAYS

☑ When it comes to your retirement, you can only count on yourself. Do not rely on factors that you cannot control.

☑ It's easy to overreact to market volatility, but pulling your money out of the market because of a downturn will cost you.

☑ Make sure you regularly rebalance your portfolio to ensure that your asset allocation continues to reflect your goals and time horizon.

☑ The money for your first three years of retirement expenses should be in a stable and conservative asset class, such as short-term bonds, money market funds, or cash equivalents.

☑ Taking money from your retirement account, either as a loan or simply as a distribution, can hurt your future financial stability. Consider your 401(k), 403(b), and IRA accounts off-limits until after you have retired and have reached a minimum of age fifty-nine-and-a-half.

☑ Healthcare will be a big expense in retirement. Make sure you budget for it.

☑ Work to pay off your consumer debt prior to retirement.

☑ Taking Social Security early could reduce your benefit by as much as 30 percent. Try to hold off on taking your benefits until you have reached your normal retirement age, or age seventy.

☑ Asking lots of questions can help you avoid being scammed.

CHAPTER 13

If You Don't Have Enough Saved

WHAT YOU'LL LEARN IN THIS CHAPTER

It may be that no matter how you look at the numbers, retirement in five years is simply not financially feasible. This chapter will explain what your options are for creating the retirement you'll feel satisfied with, even if you have to alter your time frame, the scope of your retirement plans, or your spending. You'll learn what not to do if you're staring down an unfunded retirement with only five years to go. The chapter will also offer suggestions for how to work longer or cut spending down to the bare minimum. We'll also cover what you can do if you are forced into retirement before you are ready, and ways you can continue to bring in money after you have retired. Finally, you'll learn how to create a "Plan B" retirement, so that you can feel confident of a contented retirement, no matter what your financial situation.

Many years ago, I was enrolled in a master of education program at Ohio State University that left me no time for doing many of the things I loved—including writing. My undergraduate alma mater, Kenyon College, offers summer creative writing programs for adults and teens, and I was determined to attend the adult workshop after completing my degree. After a long year and a half of pedagogy I felt as if I needed to regain some of my equilibrium.

The problem was that I could not figure out how I could swing the $2,000 price tag for the two-week program. I had been living on a shoestring to be able to afford my graduate degree, and no matter how creatively I looked at my budget, I couldn't figure out how to scrape together the money for the program. I called my father for advice.

After listening patiently to my plight, he said gently, "It sounds to me like you just can't afford it."

It was exactly the splash of cold water I needed.

While I have always been very money-savvy and able to make rational and clear-eyed decisions about my finances, my overwhelming desire to attend the Kenyon program had blinded me to the simple fact that it couldn't happen on my budget.

I tell this story to explain why I might have to renege on the promise I made in the introduction. I said that you will be able to retire in five years—and for many readers, that is true. However, if you are like the 13 percent of Americans age sixty or older who have absolutely no retirement savings set aside, being able to retire in five years may be out of reach.

That is not to say that those who haven't saved enough are doomed to work for the rest of their lives—or even for another ten years. It just means that you might have to adjust your expectations of what your retirement will look like. That could mean anything from deciding to transition to a different job or career after you retire from your primary career, to learning how to live a good life on significantly less than you planned.

Before you start lamenting the loss of retirement as you've always dreamed of it, remember that such expectation shifts can often turn out to be a really good thing. They may give you a new perspective and turn you in an unexpected but welcome direction.

So, if you are reading this book because you have no or very little money saved and you want to retire in five years, there is no magic bullet that will allow you to have it all. But if you can revise your expectations about your life before and after retirement, you can still enjoy a fulfilling life post-career. It just means you have to face the harsh truth: You might not be able to afford the retirement you've always wanted in the exact time frame you'd prefer.

Ignoring that truth will not make the situation any easier for you. Throughout this chapter, we'll talk about the options available to you if you have not saved enough. While some of these options may seem unpalatable, each one can put you in a much better position to have a retirement that looks like the one you've planned.

What Not to Do

Before getting into the details of what you can do to prepare for retirement if you have insufficient savings, we should take a moment to talk about what you absolutely should not do: Take risks in order to catch up.

As we discussed in Chapter 12, desperation can make near-retirees very vulnerable to scams and bad advice. Just because a salesperson, financial adviser, or product promoter is telling you what you want to hear does not make it true.

In particular, you may be tempted to load up your portfolio with aggressive stocks to attempt to make up for the missed years of compound interest. But this is about as sound a strategy as taking your money to Vegas. Yes, you might luck out and earn enough growth in the next five years to still be able to retire on time and in the style you want. However, it's more likely that you'll lose out from this strategy. If the market takes a sudden downturn, or even if the stocks don't perform as well as you hope, you could be in a worse position than you are right now. Similarly, get-rich-quick schemes that promise you riches for working from home, or only ask a "small upfront financial commitment" for you to reap huge benefits, can sound like the answer to a prayer. However, these types of scams are more like a nightmare. As we discussed in Chapter 12, financial scams targeting those over age sixty are a big business. Do not allow desperation to cloud your good sense.

There are no shortcuts to retirement wealth. There is no secret and no magic solution. Yes, there may be individuals who are able to play the stock market or make $5,000 a week part-time in their underwear. And world-record holder Roy Sullivan was struck by lightning seven times in his lifetime. Just because something could happen does not mean you should count on it happening to you.

It is a far better solution to plan for what is most likely. Doing that means you will have to build your wealth the old-fashioned way: by spending less, saving more, and giving your money the time it needs to grow.

Option 1: Work Longer

Let's get the most unpleasant option out of the way first. Working just a few extra years past your projected retirement date can make an enormous difference in your retirement income. There are many benefits to working longer than you planned:

1. You have more time to add to your retirement portfolios—and at the higher 50+ catch-up limits.
2. You delay drawing down your nest egg.
3. You give your investments more time to let compound interest build your wealth.
4. You can continue to use your employer's healthcare coverage.
5. You can more easily delay your Social Security benefits, meaning you will see more money once you do enroll. (See Chapter 5 for more details.)

Of course, the potential downside is that you will be working longer. If you enjoy your job and fear that you might be at loose ends when you no longer have to go to the office every morning, working a little longer can be a win-win. However, even if you are dreaming of the day you can say "So long, suckers!" to your workplace, the financial benefits of adding some time to the end of your career can make even the most hated employment situation more bearable. After all, even if you are moving your retirement date back, there is still light at the end of the tunnel.

WHAT TO DO IF YOU NEED TO DELAY RETIREMENT

Of course, putting off retirement is not necessarily as simple as deciding that you'll work longer. You may find that your employer or your health may force you to remain on your original retirement timeline. So if you decide to delay your retirement for a few years, there are several things you need to do now in order to be ready:

- Make sure you have adequate disability insurance. We discussed this in detail in Chapter 8, but it bears repeating. If you can only afford to retire if you continue to bring in a paycheck for the next five or more years, then you absolutely must insure against the possibility of losing your ability to work. Even if you are insured through your employer, double-check what benefits you can expect, and explore the option of adding some supplemental insurance.

- Talk to your HR department and your employer. You and your employer each need to know what the other expects. If your company believes that you will be retiring at a specific, predetermined date, then it may start looking for a replacement when you are considering putting off retirement for another couple of years. In addition, your HR department can help you to understand what options are available to you—including the possibility of taking a partial retirement wherein you keep working part-time or only while training a new person. Being open and honest with your employer can help you to figure out the best course of action.

- Keep networking. There is always the possibility that you will not be able to continue working in your current position, and finding a new job so late in your career can be a difficult task. But do not forget just how much experience and knowledge you bring to the table—experience and knowledge that others would be happy to learn from. If you stay current with both your social and professional networks, you increase the chances of finding an alternative to your job if you find yourself involuntarily retired.

Protecting your job (and your paycheck) is only a part of what you need to do to prepare for a delayed retirement. The other important factor is making sure that you amp up your retirement savings to maximize the impact of your additional working years.

For many, it can seem as though there is no way to squeeze any more blood from the turnip. But the truth is that you will not miss money you don't see, and small amounts add up. Start by increasing your 401(k) contribution by 1 percent. After three or four months, increase it another 1 percent. Continue doing this until you have (at least) reached the employer contribution-matching amount, but ideally until you have maxed out the contribution limit. (See Chapter 2 for more details on maxing out your retirement savings.)

Finally, while you are gearing up for some extra years before retirement, take a hard look at your current budget and lifestyle. If there are expenses that you can cut now to shorten the extra time you need to work, that can be an excellent tradeoff. Even if slashing your spending doesn't mean you'll be able to retire on time, it can make a big difference in your quality of life post-retirement. (See Chapter 2 on ways to reduce your pre-retirement budget, and see Worksheet 2–4, re-created later in this chapter, to find specific ways to cut your expenses.)

WHAT IF YOU ARE FORCED TO RETIRE?

When my mother was sixty-one years old, she contracted acute pneumonia and had to be placed in a chemically induced coma for several weeks in order to heal. Once she recovered from the pneumonia and woke up from her coma, it took more than six months of rehabilitation for her to relearn how to do many basic functions, like eating and walking. A year and a half after her ordeal began, she was back to her usual vibrant and healthy self, for which we were all exceedingly grateful.

However, her career was one casualty of her illness. My mother owned her own business—an art gallery—for nearly forty years. Unfortunately, it was not able to survive without her at the helm. This experience made it abundantly clear to me that even healthy and young individuals can suffer devastating career setbacks. For those who are within five years of retirement (or who are planning on delaying retirement), there are several things you can do in order to protect your finances from such a setback.

1. **SET UP A SECOND INCOME STREAM.** It's an important strategy for ensuring your income, no matter the status of your career. Many second income streams are active—second jobs, consulting work, and so forth—which could make them harder to maintain if you are forced to retire for health reasons. However, passive income streams, such as rent coming in from a boarder, could help you through tough times no matter the underlying cause.

2. **DISABILITY INSURANCE.** Not to beat a dead horse, but I cannot overstate the importance of this insurance. See Chapter 8 for details.

3. **NEGOTIATE IF YOU'RE LAID OFF.** If your employer is forcing you to retire early, don't be afraid to be very assertive in your severance requests. Federal age discrimination laws require that employers provide workers who are over age forty at least twenty-one days to review a termination agreement or severance package before the worker has to sign it. Use that time to figure out your financial and healthcare needs without the job and ask for them. While group layoffs often have less wiggle room for this type of negotiation, it's still a good idea to try, especially if you have a long history with the company.

4. **COME UP WITH A "PLAN B" RETIREMENT.** An important step in the retirement planning process is determining your bare minimum for living a satisfying life in retirement. While you certainly can and should dream big for your golden years, it's also crucial to recognize what parts of your dream you can give up and still live a happy and comfortable life. We'll talk more about creating a Plan B retirement later in this chapter.

There are no guarantees in this life, and so part of your retirement planning should include plans for how to handle a less-than-ideal beginning to your retirement.

Option 2: Generate Income in Retirement

If you are unwilling or unable to continue working in your current position beyond your projected retirement date, there are plenty of ways to retire from your career and still bring in a paycheck. This can not only help you to cover your living expenses in retirement without having to overtax your savings or enroll in Social Security before the optimal time, but it can also have enormous psychological benefits. The transition from career to retirement can often be a difficult one, and finding either part-time or freelance work can do a great deal to stave off depression, which plagues many retirees. According to a report by the Institute of Economic Affairs, retirement increases the risk of clinical depression by 40 percent. The solution, according to this report? Work longer. Basically, generating extra income in retirement will help your finances and your quality of life.

There are a number of options for keeping the income flowing after ending your career: Continuing to work in the same field after you retire is one excellent way to put your years of experience to use. Your employer may be interested in having you work part-time or as a consultant, which will keep you feeling connected to your work and your colleagues. Another option is to take whatever you did full-time before your retirement and find a way to either become a freelancer or work independently. This will allow you to create your own flexible schedule and choose the projects that most interest you.

If you'd prefer a more traditional part-time job, look for opportunities where you're going to be anyway. For instance, if you love to golf and know you'll be playing regularly, look for part-time positions at your local golf course. Not only will that help you increase your retirement income, but it will also reduce your expenses since you'll be able to golf for free.

Other options along those lines include working for a college if you'd like to take classes while you are retired. With the economy heading more toward part-time jobs, you should be able to find a fun part-time working experience where you know you'll already be spending time.

It all comes down to keeping an open mind. You will feel both younger and more empowered if you allow yourself to come up with creative ways to generate income that still allow you to enjoy your post-career life.

Option 3: Cut Your Spending to the Bone

As mentioned many times throughout this book, the only things you have control over in planning your retirement are how much you spend and how much you save. If you're looking at an enormous shortfall in your retirement savings, it may be time to go back to your pre-retirement budget from Chapter 2 and find other expenses you can cut from your budget.

One good way to do this is to look at your retirement shortfall from Worksheet 1–1, and figure out what you would need to put away each month in order to make it up. Then, with that figure in mind, go back over your working budget and trim anything and everything you can in order to ensure you have the necessary shortfall amount each month. This can end up being a fairly extreme solution. You may find that you and your spouse have to go down to one car, downsize your home, stop eating at restaurants, and cancel your yearly vacations in order to find the extra money in the budget to cover your savings shortfall. However, as financial adviser Alexey Bulankov puts it, "Paying yourself first means putting money aside for retirement goals before meeting all other obligations—including monthly bills."

While no one enjoys having to scale back, if you remember to focus on what this sacrifice will allow you to do in retirement, it can be much easier to bear.

In addition, getting used to a lower standard of living now can help you ensure your money goes further in retirement. For instance, you may find that living without cable or a cell phone data plan actually improves your quality of life while also reducing your expenses. Cutting your expenses now may help you realize you don't need many of the things you have long thought of as necessities. You can bring that minimalist sensibility to your retirement, which will help to stretch your retirement income.

To help determine what you can cut and by how much, let's revisit Worksheet 2–4: Reworking Your Expenses, from Chapter 2. This time, though, focus on cutting absolutely everything that you can. You can use the budgeting worksheets from Chapter 2 (specifically Worksheet 2–1 and Worksheet 2–2) to help you fill out this worksheet:

WORKSHEET 2-4:
Reworking Your Expenses

EXPENSE	CURRENT AMOUNT	WAYS TO REDUCE	NEW AMOUNT
Groceries/household items	$		$
Entertainment	$		$
Dining out	$		$
Laundry/dry cleaning	$		$

EXPENSE	CURRENT AMOUNT	WAYS TO REDUCE	NEW AMOUNT
Gas/tolls/parking	$		$
Public transportation	$		$
Church/charitable contributions	$		$
Postage and office supplies	$		$
Walk-around money	$		$
Mortgage/rent	$		$
Car payment/lease	$		$
Electric bill	$		$
Gas bill	$		$
Water bill	$		$
Sewer bill	$		$
Trash pickup bill	$		$
Cable/Internet/satellite bill	$		$
Telephone bill	$		$
Cell phone bill	$		$
Bank charges	$		$
Personal care	$		$
Home equity loan	$		$
Other loans	$		$
Credit card bill	$		$
Clothing	$		$
Medical expenses	$		$
Memberships	$		$
Car maintenance	$		$
Home maintenance	$		$

EXPENSE	CURRENT AMOUNT	WAYS TO REDUCE	NEW AMOUNT
Tuition	$		$
Nonholiday gifts	$		$
Auto insurance	$		$
Property taxes	$		$
Homeowner's/renter's insurance	$		$
Vehicle registration	$		$
Car repair	$		$
Home repair	$		$
Holiday gifts	$		$
Vacation	$		$
Total expenses that cannot change (includes child support and alimony)	$		$
TOTAL	$		$

If you can find ways to cut enough of your expenses now, even if it means drastically changing your living standards, you might still be able to retire in the five-year time frame you'd prefer.

Option 4: Create a "Plan B" Retirement

The final method for dealing with insufficient savings requires you to think about the worst-case scenario for your money. If you are unable to save enough to continue your current lifestyle, what kind of life in retirement are you willing to accept? You need to figure out what kind of Plan B you can live with if the money simply isn't there.

In order to create your Plan B retirement plan, sit down with your financial adviser and determine what your monthly and/or yearly income would be in retirement based on your current savings and the amount that you will be able to put away in the next five years. Once you've gotten over your shock at the low number, it's time to start figuring out how you would live on that amount. What changes could you make to your life? What changes are you unwilling to make? What is the bare minimum necessary for your happiness?

YOU PROBABLY NEED LESS THAN YOU THINK YOU DO

You may find that security and happiness require a lot less capital than you think they do. For instance, an elderly retiree of my acquaintance did not save enough before she and her husband retired, and then their portfolio took a major hit in the 2008 downturn. After becoming a widow, she lived out the rest of her life quite happily in a group home for low-income seniors. She said that as long as she had a safe place to rest her head, enough food to eat, and plenty of books to read (thanks to the local library), she was satisfied with her life.

It would be very helpful for everyone to think through what his or her bare minimum requirements are for life satisfaction. Such an exercise can help take some of the pressure off of you in planning for retirement—as in, even under the worst-case financial scenario, you know that you'll still be able to do X, Y, or Z that are most important to you.

Taking the time to run the worst-case scenario numbers with your financial adviser now can also be enough of a spur to get you to make changes in your current spending habits to improve your retirement outlook. At the very least, it will insulate you from the shock of having to seriously downgrade your lifestyle after retirement. You will know far in advance that your lifestyle will change when you stop working, and it will give you time to either acclimate to the idea or make changes to your retirement savings, your spending, or your overall plan in order to avoid it.

In order to help you figure out what your bare minimum necessities are for a comfortable life in retirement, let's revisit Worksheet 11–1: What Will My Retirement Look Like? from Chapter 11. This time, instead of filling in your ideal retirement plans, describe the minimum retirement lifestyle you will need:

WORKSHEET 11-1:

What Will My Retirement Look Like?

1. Describe a typical day post-retirement.

   YOU: ....

   ....

   YOUR SPOUSE: ....

   ....

2. Describe a typical week post-retirement.

   YOU: ....

   ....

   YOUR SPOUSE: ....

   ....

3. Describe a typical month post-retirement.

   YOU: ....

   ....

   YOUR SPOUSE: ....

   ....

4. Describe a typical year post-retirement.

   YOU: ....

   ....

   YOUR SPOUSE: ....

   ....

With your reduced retirement expectations in mind, you can change the dollar amounts you originally filled out in Worksheet 11–3.

WORKSHEET 11-3:

Anticipated Retirement-Related Expenses

EXPENSE	AMOUNT	MULTIPLY BY	ANNUAL AMOUNT
Hobbies	$	× 12	$
Memberships (including country clubs)	$	× 12	$
Local travel	$	× 12	$
Holiday/family travel	$	× 4	$
TOTAL	$		$

The point of creating a Plan B retirement plan is to both prepare yourself for the potential major change in your lifestyle and give you the necessary information to help you figure out a way to avoid the worst-case scenario. For both reasons, it is an excellent exercise for every near-retiree, not just those who are behind in their savings.

Get Where You're Going

Whether you are comfortably set for your retirement or you haven't yet put a single penny away, it's important to sit down with the worksheets throughout this book and with your financial adviser to make sure you understand where you are and what you can do about it.

CHAPTER 13 TAKEAWAYS

☑ If you don't have enough saved, there is no magic bullet that will allow you to have the exact retirement you want in the exact time frame you prefer. Coming to terms with adjusting your retirement vision will help you make the best decisions for yourself and your finances.

☑ Trying to "make up for lost time" with aggressive investments or get-rich-quick schemes is the worst possible thing you can do if you don't have enough saved.

☑ Delaying your retirement could help you beef up your nest egg and put off taking Social Security.

☑ Retirement is not always voluntary. Disability insurance and a second income stream can help protect your income.

☑ If you are forced into retirement because of a layoff or firing, you have twenty-one days to review your termination agreement or severance package. Do not be afraid to negotiate with your former employer.

☑ Retiring from your career to take a part-time job can help you balance your retirement budget.

☑ Cutting your spending down to the bare minimum can both free up more money to send to your retirement accounts and help you get used to living on less.

☑ Create a Plan B retirement plan, which is the least you would need to feel contented in retirement. Whether you have savings or not, this exercise can help you work through the worst-case scenario and recognize that you can still have the basic things that are most important to you.

What to Do When

YEARS TO RETIREMENT	WHAT TO DO
Five	Schedule an appointment with your financial adviser to discuss the worst-case scenario and your options.
Five	Increase your 401(k) contribution by at least 1 percent.
Five	Enroll in disability insurance.
Five	Schedule an appointment with your HR department to discuss your extended work options.
Five	Within the next three months, begin cutting pre-retirement expenses (using Worksheet 2–4 re-created in this chapter as a guide).
Five	Within the next six months, work with your spouse and your financial adviser to create a Plan B retirement plan.
Five	Start generating ideas for a second income stream.
Four	Increase your 401(k) contribution by at least another 1 percent.
Four	Put your second income stream plan into action.
Four through one	Increase your 401(k) contributions by at least another 1 percent.
Four through one	Meet with your financial adviser to adjust and revise your retirement strategy.

The Retirement Readiness Checklist

WHAT WILL YOUR IDEAL RETIREMENT LOOK LIKE?

Writing down your retirement dreams will give you a goal to work toward as well as help you pinpoint what is most important to you in retirement.

Describe your typical activities in retirement from the daily to the yearly. Let your dream unfold in front of you like a movie so you can truly see what you are hoping to achieve:

DAY ....

....

WEEK ....

....

MONTH ....

....

YEAR ....

....

INCOME IN RETIREMENT

How much money will you have to live on in retirement? The following calculations can help you determine your annual retirement income:

CURRENT 401(K) OR 403(B) BALANCE	$ ....
CURRENT IRA/ROTH IRA BALANCE	+$ ....
TOTAL RETIREMENT ACCOUNT BALANCE	=$ ....
	(aka Current Principal)
ANNUAL RETIREMENT CONTRIBUTION	....
	(aka Annual Addition)
YEARS TO RETIREMENT	....
	(aka Years to Grow)
RATE OF RETURN/INTEREST RATE	....

Historically, the market earns approximately 8 percent per year, although you can assume a lower return for a more conservative estimate or a higher return for a more optimistic estimate.

CALCULATE YOUR PROJECTED NEST EGG

Enter the numbers listed previously in a compound interest calculator to determine the projected size of your nest egg as of your planned retirement date. I recommend www.moneychimp.com/calculator/compound_interest_calculator.htm as a compound interest calculator.

PROJECTED NEST EGG ....

Traditionally, you can expect to live on approximately 4 percent of your nest egg's value per year. This rule offers an easy metric for understanding your potential annual income in retirement. Dividing your projected nest egg by 25 can give you the approximate annual income you can expect in retirement:

PROJECTED NEST EGG ÷ 25 = APPROXIMATE ANNUAL INCOME IN RETIREMENT

.... ÷ 25 = ...

SOCIAL SECURITY INCOME

Your Social Security retirement benefits will be part of your retirement income. However, it is smart to calculate those benefits separately and plan for your retirement income without including Social Security. Treating your Social Security benefits as an added perk on top of your planned retirement income will help you to have a more financially stable retirement.

Creating a "my Social Security" account on the Social Security website will allow you to calculate your exact Social Security retirement benefit. The Social Security Administration no longer provides paper statements, so you must log onto "my Social Security" on the website to access your earnings record and estimated benefits: www.ssa.gov/myaccount/.

ESTIMATED MONTHLY SOCIAL SECURITY BENEFIT ....

HEALTHCARE IN RETIREMENT

Fidelity calculates that the average sixty-five-year-old couple retiring in 2020 will spend approximately $295,000 in healthcare costs in retirement.

Even though Medicare eligibility begins at age sixty-five, there are Medicare coverage gaps that can add up.

Specifically, Medicare does not cover:

- Prescription drugs
- Routine dental/eye care
- Dentures
- Hearing aids and the exams for fitting them
- Routine foot care
- Long-term care (i.e., nonmedical help that the elderly may need for daily living)

Answer the following questions:

1. What is your health insurance coverage plan in retirement?

2. Will you be eligible for Medicare as of your planned retirement date?

3. Do you have a plan for long-term care in retirement?

4. How do you currently take care of your health?

LIFE INSURANCE

Answer the following questions to determine if you will need life insurance in retirement. As of retirement:

- Will anyone depend on your income?   Y / N
- Will you carry a mortgage?   Y / N
- Will you carry other debts?   Y / N

- Will you have enough money to cover your final arrangements? **Y / N**
- Will you want your heirs to receive money immediately after your death? **Y / N**
- Will you want to leave a charitable legacy? **Y / N**

If you answered yes to any of these questions, you may want to consider options for carrying life insurance in retirement.

ESTATE PLANNING

Make sure you have made plans for what will happen to your assets in case of your death.

- Do you have a will in place? **Y / N**

- If yes, have you revisited it in the past five years? **Y / N**
  (You should plan to look over your estate plan every few years to make sure it is up to date.)

- Are the listed beneficiaries on your retirement and insurance accounts up to date? **Y / N**

- Who is the designated guardian (for minor children), trustee (to oversee any trusts), and executor (to oversee the distribution of your assets according to your will)?

    GUARDIAN ....

    TRUSTEE ....

    EXECUTOR ....

- Have you thought about how your estate plan could be thwarted based upon how it is currently written? **Y / N**

Inheritance theft is a serious problem that can affect any family. Make sure you look at your estate plan critically. An estate attorney can help you find where there may be weak spots that could be exploited to thwart your wishes. A well-written and ironclad estate plan can reassure you that no one will be fighting over your assets when you are gone.

The Five-Year Syllabus

YEARS TO RETIREMENT	WHEN TO ACT	WHAT TO DO
Five	Right now	Complete the worksheets in Chapter 1 to determine your retirement shortfall.
Five	Right now	Gather together your financial information, and complete Worksheets 2–1 through 2–5 in Chapter 2 to find ways to increase your savings.
Five	Right now	Sign up for a "my Social Security" account at www.ssa.gov/myaccount/ in order to easily access all of your Social Security records and information (see Chapter 5).
Five	Right now	If you do not currently have health insurance, visit HealthCare.gov to begin the process of enrolling in an individual healthcare plan through the ACA Health Insurance Exchange (see Chapter 8).
Five	Next month	Set up times to interview several financial advisers. Use the interview questions in Chapter 4 to find an adviser who will work well with you.
Five	Within the next three months	Implement an action plan for reducing your expenses. Worksheet 2–4 in Chapter 2 will guide you.
Five	Within the next three months	Increase your 401(k) contribution by at least 1 percent.
Five	Within the next six months	Create an action plan for paying off your consumer debt.
Five	Within the next six months	If you have enough money liquid to do so, and plan to use a deferred fixed annuity, make your purchase now to give it time to grow before you reach retirement (see Chapter 3).

YEARS TO RETIREMENT	WHEN TO ACT	WHAT TO DO
Five	By the end of the year	Decide on an adviser and meet with him or her to discuss your retirement plans and strategies. In particular, you will want to discuss: 1 Your planned withdrawal strategy (see Chapter 3) 2 Health insurance options if you plan to retire before age sixty-five (see Chapter 8) 3 Disability insurance options (see Chapter 8) 4 Long-term care insurance options (see Chapter 8) 5 Opening a Health Savings Account (see Chapter 8) 6 Opening a Roth IRA to pay for future health-care costs (see Chapter 8) 7 Creating a Plan B retirement plan if you haven't saved enough (see Chapter 13)
Five	By the end of the year	Calculate your projected Social Security benefits using the calculators at www.ssa.gov/benefits/calculators (see Chapter 5).
Five	By the end of the year	Start generating ideas for a second income stream (see Chapters 2 and 13).
Five	By the end of the year	Increase your 401(k) contribution by another 1 percent.
Four		Put your second income stream plan into action (see Chapters 2 and 13).
Four		Reassess your pre-retirement budget and make any necessary changes (see Chapter 2).
Four		Increase your 401(k) contribution by another 1 percent.
Four		If possible, max out your IRA contribution.
Four		Continue working to pay off any consumer debt. As you pay off debt, continue to send the "payment" to your retirement savings (see Chapter 2).

YEARS TO RETIREMENT	WHEN TO ACT	WHAT TO DO
Four		Meet with your financial adviser at least once this year to reassess your overall retirement strategy (see Chapter 3) and to review your Roth IRA or HSA plan for handling your health-care costs in retirement, and make any necessary adjustments to the investment strategy you have chosen together (see Chapter 8).
Four	If you have not already done so	Max out your contribution to the previous year's HSA or Roth IRA by tax day (see Chapter 8).
Four		Visit with your HR department to discuss the following: 1 The details of any disability benefits offered through your employer 2 What, if any, retirement benefits are offered through your employer 3 Request another copy of your Summary Plan Description (SPD) if you anticipate receiving retirement health benefits (see Chapter 8)
Four	If you have not already done so	Schedule an appointment with multiple insurers to check prices and enroll in disability and/or long-term care insurance (see Chapter 8).
Three		Max out your contributions to your IRA and your 401(k), if possible.
Three		Reassess your pre-retirement budget and make any necessary changes (see Chapter 2).
Three		Continue working to pay off any consumer debt. As you pay off debt, continue to send the "payment" to your retirement savings (see Chapter 2).
Three	At least once this year	Meet with your financial adviser to reassess your overall retirement strategy (see Chapter 3) and to review your Roth IRA or HSA plan for handling your healthcare costs in retirement. Make any necessary adjustments to the investment strategy you have chosen together (see Chapter 8).
Three	If you have not already done so	Max out your contribution to the previous year's HSA or Roth IRA by tax day (see Chapter 8).

YEARS TO RETIREMENT	WHEN TO ACT	WHAT TO DO
Two		Have your mortgage paid off by this year, if possible.
Two		Reassess your pre-retirement budget and make any necessary changes (see Chapter 2).
Two	By the end of this year	Try to have all consumer debt paid off.
Two		Max out your contribution to your IRA and your 401(k), if possible.
Two		Meet with your financial adviser at least once this year to reassess your overall retirement strategy (see Chapter 3) and to review your Roth IRA or HSA plan for handling your health-care costs in retirement. Make any necessary adjustments to the investment strategy you have chosen together (see Chapter 8).
Two	If you have not already done so	Max out your contribution to the previous year's HSA or Roth IRA by tax day (see Chapter 8).
One		Reassess your pre-retirement budget and make any necessary changes. Now is the time to start transitioning from your pre-retirement to your post-retirement budget (see Chapters 2 and 11).
One		Max out your contribution to your IRA and your 401(k), if possible.
One		Purchase an immediate annuity this year if you plan to use one (see Chapter 3).
One		Plan to meet with your financial adviser multiple times this year (quarterly is a good idea) to discuss: 1 Your withdrawal strategy 2 Your tax strategy 3 Your long-term investments 4 Your Roth IRA or HSA plan for handling healthcare in retirement (see Chapter 8)

YEARS TO RETIREMENT	WHEN TO ACT	WHAT TO DO
One	If you have not already done so	Max out your contribution to the previous year's HSA or Roth IRA by tax day (see Chapter 8).
One		Schedule a meeting with a representative of your HR department to discuss: 1 If and how your benefits will change if you will be receiving retirement healthcare benefits from your employer. If you've lost it, request another copy of your Summary Plan Description (SPD) (see Chapter 8) 2 What you will need to do in order to sign up for COBRA if you will not be receiving retirement healthcare benefits (see Chapter 8) 3 When your benefits will officially lapse if you will not be receiving retirement healthcare benefits (see Chapter 8)
One	If you are retiring prior to age sixty-five	Visit HealthCare.gov to begin the process of enrolling in an individual healthcare plan through the ACA Health Insurance Exchange (see Chapter 8).
One	Three months before you would like to start receiving Social Security retirement benefits	Apply for your Social Security retirement benefits online at www.socialsecurity.gov. You will need your Social Security number, your original birth certificate, proof of US citizenship, your military discharge papers if you served, and a copy of your W-2 forms or your self-employment tax return for the previous year (see Chapter 5).

The Age-Based Syllabus

YOUR AGE	WHAT TO DO
Fifty-nine-and-a-half	You may begin to make penalty-free withdrawals from your tax-sheltered accounts (including Roth and traditional IRAs and 401(k)s) if you have held them for at least five years (see Chapters 3 and 6).
Sixty-two	This is the earliest you can begin receiving Social Security retirement benefits. However, your benefits will be permanently reduced (see Chapter 5).
Sixty-four and nine months	Enroll in Medicare Part A and Part B. The initial enrollment period for Medicare spans from the three months prior to your sixty-fifth birthday, the month of your birthday, and the three months following your birthday. Missing this enrollment window will be expensive (see Chapter 7).
Sixty-four and nine months	If you choose to enroll in a Medicare Advantage Plan and/or a Medicare prescription drug plan, you can do so at the same time you enroll in Parts A and B. There is no penalty for joining a Medicare Advantage Plan at a later date, but there is if you join a prescription drug plan after this initial enrollment period (see Chapter 7).
Sixty-five	If you are planning on purchasing a Medigap policy, do so within six months of reaching age sixty-five and enrolling in Medicare Part B. Miss this window, and you will have to go through medical underwriting to qualify for a Medigap plan (see Chapter 8).
Sixty-six to sixty-seven	Depending on what year you were born, you will reach normal retirement age sometime between sixty-six and sixty-seven, at which point you will receive your full Social Security benefits (see Chapter 5).
Seventy	Every year you delay Social Security benefits between your normal retirement age and age seventy, you will see an 8 percent increase in your benefits (see Chapter 5).
Seventy-two	You must begin taking required minimum distributions from your 401(k) and your traditional IRA (see Chapter 3).

BIBLIOGRAPHY

"2020 Employer Health Benefits Survey—Summary of Findings." Kaiser Family Foundation, October 8, 2020. *http://files.kff.org/attachment/Summary-of-Findings-Employer-Health-Benefits-2020.pdf.*

"401(k) Contribution Limit Increases to $19,500 for 2020; Catch-Up Limit Rises to $6,500." Internal Revenue Service, November 6, 2019. *www.irs.gov/newsroom/401k-contribution-limit-increases-to-19500-for-2020-catch-up-limit-rises-to-6500.*

"Amount of Roth IRA Contributions That You Can Make for 2020." Internal Revenue Service. Accessed December 14, 2020. *www.irs.gov/retirement-plans/plan-participant-employee/amount-of-roth-ira-contributions-that-you-can-make-for-2020.*

Annuity Digest. "Types of Financial Advisors." *www.annuitydigest.com/best-annuity/types-financial-advisors.*

Anspach, Dana. "How to Evaluate the Cost of Hiring a Financial Planner." *The Balance,* July 17, 2020. *www.thebalance.com/ways-financial-advisors-charge-fees-2388441.*

Araujo, Mila. "Preventive Services Covered by Medicare." *The Balance,* January 31, 2020. *www.thebalance.com/preventative-services-covered-by-medicare-4161301.*

Bach, David. *Smart Women Finish Rich, Expanded and Updated.* New York: Crown Publishing Group, 2018.

Bell, Kay, and Tina Orem. "Estate Tax: Definition, Tax Rates and Who Pays in 2020–2021." *NerdWallet,* November 14, 2020. *www.nerdwallet.com/blog/taxes/which-states-have-estate-inheritance-taxes/.*

Birken, Emily Guy. "How the CARES Act Eases Retirement Account Rules During COVID-19." *Forbes,* July 6, 2020. *www.forbes.com/advisor/retirement/cares-act-retirement-account-rules-covid-19/.*

———. *Making Social Security Work for You: Advice, Strategies, and Timelines That Can Maximize Your Benefits.* Avon, MA: Adams Media, 2016.

Centers for Disease Control. "Table 22. Life Expectancy at Birth, at Age 65, and at Age 75, by Sex, Race, and Hispanic Origin: United States, Selected Years 1900–2010." *www.cdc.gov/nchs/data/hus/2011/022.pdf.*

Chatzky, Jean. "Do You Need Disability Insurance?" AARP, August 23, 2012. *www.aarp.org/health/health-insurance/info-08-2012/disability-insurance-do-you-need-it.2.html.*

Coombes, Andrea. "8 Tips to Trim Your Retirement Tax Bill." *MarketWatch*, April 12, 2013. *www.marketwatch.com/story/8-tips-to-trim-your-retirement-tax-bill-2013-04-12.*

Copeland, Craig. "Who Is Most Vulnerable to the Ticking Debt Time Bomb in Retirement: Families with the Oldest, Black/African American, and Hispanic Family Heads." Employee Benefit Research Institute, December 17, 2020. *www.ebri.org/content/who-is-most-vulnerable-to-the-ticking-debt-time-bomb-in-retirement-families-with-the-oldest-black-african-american-and-hispanic-family-heads.*

"Cost of Care Survey." Genworth. *www.genworth.com/aging-and-you/finances/cost-of-care.html.*

"Costs in the Coverage Gap." Medicare. *www.medicare.gov/drug-coverage-part-d/costs-for-medicare-drug-coverage/costs-in-the-coverage-gap.*

"Costs of Care." LongTermCare.gov. US Department of Health and Human Services. *https://longtermcare.acl.gov/costs-how-to-pay/costs-of-care.html.*

Deane, Stephen. "Elder Financial Exploitation." US Securities and Exchange Commission, June 2018. *www.sec.gov/files/elder-financial-exploitation.pdf.*

Dowd, Casey. "Boomers: Avoid These Retirement Pitfalls." *Fox Business*, November 17, 2011. *www.foxbusiness.com/features/boomers-avoid-these-retirement-pitfalls.*

Ebeling, Ashlea. "IRS Announces Higher Estate and Gift Tax Limits for 2020." *Forbes*, November 6, 2019. *www.forbes.com/sites/ashleaebeling/2019/11/06/irs-announces-higher-estate-and-gift-tax-limits-for-2020/#71fba0782efb.*

El-Sibaie, Amir. "2021 Tax Brackets." Tax Foundation, October 27, 2020. *https://taxfoundation.org/2021-tax-brackets/.*

"Everything You Need to Know about the DOL Fiduciary Rule." *Investopedia*, December 19, 2019. *www.investopedia.com/updates/dol-fiduciary-rule/.*

"Explaining Health Care Reform: Questions about Health Insurance Subsidies." Kaiser Family Foundation, October 30, 2020. *www.kff.org/health-reform/issue-brief/explaining-health-care-reform-questions-about-health-insurance-subsidies/.*

Farrington, Robert. "Capital Gains Tax Brackets 2021: What They Are and Rates." *The College Investor*, October 26, 2020. *https://thecollegeinvestor.com/23577/capital-gains-tax-brackets/.*

Friedberg, Leora, Wenliang Hou, Wei Sun, and Anthony Webb. "Long-Term Care: How Big a Risk?" Center for Retirement Research at Boston College, November 2014. *https://crr.bc.edu/briefs/long-term-care-how-big-a-risk/.*

Granger, Amelia. "When You Haven't Saved Enough for Retirement." *Next Avenue*, May 13, 2013. *www.nextavenue.org/what-do-if-you-havent-saved-enough-retirement/.*

Hebeler, Henry K. "Free Computer Programs." *Analyze Now! www.analyzenow.com/Free%20Programs/free_programs.htm.*

"High Deductible Health Plan (HDHP)." HealthCare.gov. *www.healthcare.gov/glossary/high-deductible-health-plan/.*

"Housing America's Older Adults 2019." Joint Center for Housing of Harvard University. *www.jchs.harvard.edu/sites/default/files/Harvard_JCHS_Housing_Americas_Older_Adults_2019.pdf.*

"How Continuing Care Retirement Communities Work." AARP, October 24, 2019. *www.aarp.org/caregiving/basics/info-2017/continuing-care-retirement-communities.html.*

"How Much Care Will You Need?" LongTermCare.gov. US Department of Health and Human Services. *https://longtermcare.acl.gov/the-basics/how-much-care-will-you-need.html.*

"How to Compare Medigap Policies." Medicare.gov. *www.medicare.gov/supplements-other-insurance/how-to-compare-medigap-policies.*

"How to Plan for Rising Healthcare Costs." Fidelity, August 3, 2020. *www.fidelity.com/viewpoints/personal-finance/plan-for-rising-health-care-costs.*

Iacurci, Greg. "More People May Soon Have Annuities in Their 401(k) Plans." CNBC, January 3, 2020. *www.cnbc.com/2020/01/03/more-people-may-soon-have-annuities-in-their-401k-plans.html.*

"Internal Revenue Bulletin: 2019–22." Internal Revenue Service, May 28, 2019. *www.irs.gov/pub/irs-irbs/irb19-22.pdf.*

Irby, LaToya. "The 8 Best Personal Finance Software Options of 2020." *The Balance*, September 16, 2020. *www.thebalance.com/best-personal-finance-software-4171938.*

IRS Publication 915: "Social Security and Equivalent Railroad Retirement Benefits." Internal Revenue Service. *www.irs.gov/pub/irs-pdf/p915.pdf.*

Jason, Julie. *The AARP Retirement Survival Guide: How to Make Smart Financial Decisions in Good Times and Bad.* New York: Sterling Publishing, 2009.

Kunkle Roberts, Danielle. "How Much Do Medigap Plans Cost?" *Forbes*, February 6, 2018. *www.forbes.com/sites/forbesfinancecouncil/2018/02/06/how-much-do-medigap-plans-cost/#276943ad2dfa.*

Kurt, Daniel. "What Is the SECURE Act and How Could It Affect Your Retirement?" *Investopedia*, March 31, 2020. *www.investopedia.com/what-is-secure-act-how-affect-retirement-4692743.*

Levine, Jeffrey. "How Required Minimum Distribution (RMD) Changes under the SECURE Act Impact Retirement Accounts." Kitces.com, February 5, 2020. *www.kitces.com/blog/secure-act-age-72-required-minimum-distribution-rmd-age-70-1-2-qcd-2020/.*

"Lifetime Reserve Days." Medicare Interactive. *www.medicareinteractive.org/get-answers/medicare-covered-services/inpatient-hospital-services/lifetime-reserve-days.*

"Long-Term Care Insurance Policy Costs—2018." American Association for Long-Term Care Insurance. *www.aaltci.org/long-term-care-insurance/learning-center/ltcfacts.php#costs.*

Marotta, David John. "The False Promises of Annuities and Annuity Calculators." *Forbes*, August 27, 2012. *www.forbes.com/sites/davidmarotta/2012/08/27/ the-false-promises-of-annuities-and-annuity-calculators/?sh=6ccaf9f0529d*.

"Medicare & You." Medicare.gov. *www.medicare.gov/medicare-and-you*.

Nationwide Retirement Institute, June 26, 2018. *www.nationwide.com/personal/ about-us/newsroom/press-release?title=062618-nf-healthcare-survey*.

"Part A Late Enrollment Penalty." Medicare.gov. *www.medicare.gov/your-medicare-costs/ part-a-costs/part-a-late-enrollment-penalty*.

"Phases of Part D Coverage." Medicare Interactive. *www.medicareinteractive. org/get-answers/medicare-prescription-drug-coverage-part-d/medicare-part-d-costs/ phases-of-part-d-coverage*.

Pogol, Gina. "Preparing to Buy a Home: True Cost of Home Ownership." HSH.com, August 13, 2019. *www.hsh.com/first-time-homebuyer/cost-of-owning-a-house.html*.

Renzulli, Kerri Anne. "This Is How Much Debt the Average American Has Now— at Every Age." *Money*, April 13, 2018. *https://money.com/average-debt-every-age/*.

"Report on the Economic Well-Being of US Households in 2018." Board of Governors of the Federal Reserve System, May 2019. *www.federalreserve.gov/ publications/files/2018-report-economic-well-being-us-households-201905.pdf*.

"Retirement Benefits: Access, Participation, and Take-up Rates." US Bureau of Labor Statistics. *www.bls.gov/ncs/ebs/benefits/2018/ownership/private/table02a.htm*.

"Retirement & Survivors Benefits: Life Expectancy Calculator." Social Security Administration. Accessed December 14, 2020. *www.ssa.gov/oact/population/ longevity.html*.

"Retirement Topics—IRA Contribution Limits." Internal Revenue Service. Accessed December 14, 2020. *www.irs.gov/retirement-plans/plan-participant-employee/ retirement-topics-ira-contribution-limits*.

Sahlgren, Gabriel H. "Work Longer, Live Healthier." Institute of Economic Affairs, May 2013. *www.iea.org.uk*.

Schoeff, Mark, Jr. "It's Official: DOL Fiduciary Rule Is Dead." *InvestmentNews*, June 21, 2018. *www.investmentnews.com/article/20180621/FREE/180629985/ its-official-dol-fiduciary-rule-is-dead*.

Singer, Mark. "Four Types of Financial Planning Professionals." *Your Retirement Journey*, January 16, 2013. *www.yourretirementjourney.com/ post/1402262-four-types-of-financial-planning-professionals*.

Social Security Administration. "Exempt Amounts under the Earnings Test." *www.ssa.gov/oact/cola/rtea.html*.

Social Security Administration. "OASDI and SSI Program Rates & Limits, 2020." *www.ssa.gov/policy/docs/quickfacts/prog_highlights/RatesLimits2020.html*.

Social Security Administration. "Quarter of Coverage." *www.ssa.gov/oact/cola/QC.html*.

Social Security Administration. "Social Security Announces 1.3 Percent Benefit Increase for 2021," October 13, 2020. *www.ssa.gov/news/press/releases/2020/*.

Social Security Administration. "Fact Sheet: Social Security." *www.ssa.gov/news/press/factsheets/basicfact-alt.pdf.*

Social Security Administration. "A Summary of the 2020 Annual Reports." Accessed December 14, 2020. *www.ssa.gov/oact/TRSUM/*.

Stouffer, Tere. *The Only Budgeting Book You'll Ever Need.* Avon, MA: Adams Media, 2012.

Urken, Ross Kenneth. "Forget the 4% Rule: Retirement's Common Wisdom Is Obsolete." AOL.com, March 26, 2012. *www.aol.com/2012/03/26/forget-the-4-rule-retirements-common-wisdom-is-obsolete/*.

US Department of Labor. "Can the Retiree Health Benefits Provided by Your Employer Be Cut?" *www.dol.gov/sites/dolgov/files/ebsa/about-ebsa/our-activities/resource-center/publications/can-the-retiree-health-benefits-be-cut.pdf.*

"US Transfer Activity, Policy & Cost." Worldwide ERC. *https://arcrelocation.com/wp-content/uploads/2018/02/2016-ARC-US-Transfer-and-Cost-Survey.pdf.*

Watson, Garrett, Huaqun Li, and Taylor LaJoie. "Details and Analysis of President Joe Biden's Tax Plan," October 22, 2020. Tax Foundation. *https://taxfoundation.org/joe-biden-tax-plan-2020/*.

"What Does Original Medicare Cost?" MedicareResources.org, February 12, 2020. *www.medicareresources.org/faqs/what-does-original-medicare-cost-the-beneficiary/*.

"What Do Social Security Taxes Pay For?" InCharge Debt Solutions. *www.incharge.org/financial-literacy/where-do-my-social-security-tax-dollars-go/*.

Wiatrowski, William J. "Changing Landscape of Employment-Based Retirement Benefits." US Bureau of Labor Statistics: Compensation and Working Conditions, September 29, 2011. *www.bls.gov/opub/mlr/cwc/changing-landscape-of-employment-based-retirement-benefits.pdf.*

INDEX

ABOUT THE AUTHOR

EMILY GUY BIRKEN is a former educator, lifelong money nerd, and a Plutus Award–winning freelance writer who specializes in the scientific research behind irrational money behaviors. Her background in education allows her to make complex financial topics relatable and easily understood by the layperson. Her work has appeared on *HuffPost*, *Business Insider*, *Kiplinger*, *MSN Money*, *Forbes*, and *The Washington Post* online, and she has appeared in *Woman's Day*, *Real Simple*, *Redbook*, and *Woman's World*. Emily lives in Milwaukee with an absentminded engineer, two children who are determined to make her an expert on Pokémon, a misbehaving greyhound, and a cat that often doubles as a throw pillow.

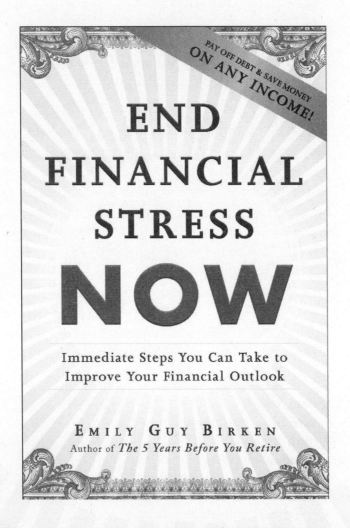